THE SPORTING CLAYS HANDBOOK

THE
Sporting Clays
HANDBOOK

·

———

JERRY MEYER

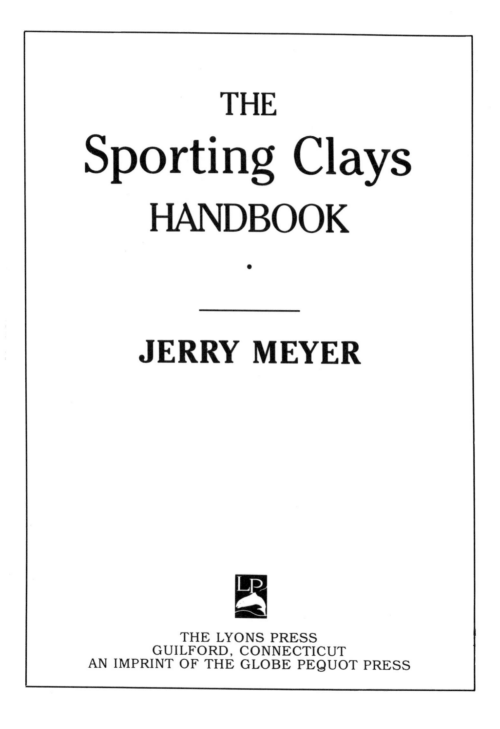

THE LYONS PRESS
GUILFORD, CONNECTICUT
AN IMPRINT OF THE GLOBE PEQUOT PRESS

The photographs on pages 2, 4, 9, 19, 38, 70, 78, 82, and 139 are used by kind permission of George Conrad/*Sporting Clays* magazine.

The Lyons Press is an imprint of The Globe Pequot Press.

Library of Congress Cataloging-in-Publication Data

Meyer, Jerry, 1939–
    The sporting clays handbook / Jerry Meyer.
        p.   cm.
    ISBN 1-55821-066-0
    1. Trapshooting. I. Title.
GV1181.M44 1990
799.2'13—dc20   90-34138
                              CIP

Manufactured in the United States of America
First edition/Tenth printing

This one is for the kids,

Chris, Amy, Sarah, Johnny,

and my first grandperson,

who is scheduled for publication at about the same time

as this book.

CONTENTS

•

ACKNOWLEDGMENTS

•

It is impossible to write a book without a lot of help from a lot of friends. Many of my friends have been of invaluable assistance in providing information, posing for pictures, and loaning products for testing and research.

In an effort to provide the reader with a wide range of information on sporting clays, I have interviewed, shot with, and taken lessons from most of the better shooters in this country. This volume would have been very limited in scope if I had relied entirely on my personal experiences over the past few years. A list of shooters who have made a major contribution to this book would have to include: Jon Kruger, King Howington, Holly Haggard, Cheng Ma, Chappie Gennett, Dave Bleha, Bobby Jernigan, Bob Brister, Jim Maier, Andy Folsom, Skip Hoagland, Gale Davis, Dan Mitchell, Bud Ward, Ken Hoover, Lauren Blackmon, Sue King, Andy Duffy, Mike Hampton, Sid Dykes, Sandy Wood, Ken Gagnon.

Every sporting clays course I shot on in the past months was extremely helpful in answering questions and sharing ideas on designing sporting clays fields. If you are near any of the following courses, I recommend you shoot a few rounds; I did and enjoyed myself thoroughly. Cherokee Rose Plantation, Griffin, Georgia; Game Hill Hunting Club, Weston, Missouri; Heartbreak Ridge, Albany, Georgia; Minnesota

Horse and Hunt Club, Prior Lake, Minnesota; Myrtlewood Plantation, Thomasville, Georgia; NSSA National Gun Club, San Antonio, Texas; Pigeon Mountain Sporting Clays, Chickamauga, Georgia; Rocky Comfort Sporting Clays, Quincy, Florida; South River Gun Club, Covington, Georgia; Wolf Creek Gun Club, Atlanta, Georgia.

These manufacturers were generous in providing products for testing and technical data for inclusion in this book: Barbour Clothing, Beretta, Bob Allen, Browning, Champion E.T. Traps, Champion Targets, Federal Cartridge, Listo Traps, Ranging, Inc., Remington, Shooting Academy, Jim White's Stick Birds, White Flyer Targets, Winchester.

The list would not be complete without a bunch of other folks who provided time, talent, and information: George Conrad, Lois Lessing, Brian Skeuse, Richard Grozik, Bob Corsetti, Greg Foster, Mike Davey, Robert Fancher, Jr., Jay Bunting, Jr., David Miller, Jr., Austin Bell, Mike Larsen, Karen Crosby.

Without a doubt, the greatest debt of gratitude goes to Nick Lyons, who believed in this book enough to publish it.

INTRODUCTION

•

Sporting clays is experiencing a phenomenal growth in the United States. Many shooters, after trying the sport for the first time, become instant addicts and want to learn more about sporting clays. Every new sporting clays enthusiast has the same questions. Which guns are best for shooting sporting clays? What are the best loads and chokes for the various fields? What are the basic techniques for shooting from the low-gun ready-position? How do you shoot the various fields? Where can I find descriptions for fields such as fur and feather, driven pheasant, driven grouse, springing teal, wood pigeon, settling woodies, and decoying mallards? Where can I get a translation for such terms as report pair, true pair, following pair, European rotation, midi, mini, rocket, battue, and poison birds?

The sole purpose of this book is to answer these and the many other questions of the new sporting clays shooter. Special care has been exercised to provide the new shooter with basic information on how this exciting shotgun sport is played. Suggestions on guns, ammo, and chokes are provided to assist in making decisions.

I hope this book will help you enjoy the fun and excitement of this fast-growing sport. Writing this book has required me to spend a lot more time on my dang computer than on sporting clays courses during the past year. But that is about to change. If you call the house and don't get an answer—I'll be out shooting sporting clays!

1

SPORTING CLAYS

A Description of the Game

•

Shotgunners in the United States are in the enjoyable position of having a new sport bloom before their very eyes, and many are becoming active participants. It has taken nearly half a century for sporting clays to cross the Atlantic and become popular in the United States. But after a slow start the sport is enjoying phenomenal growth with new sporting clay facilities opening and numbers of shooters increasing by the hundreds each month.

On any given weekend or holiday in England there will be literally hundreds of opportunities for shooters to participate in a sporting clays tournament. There are nearly a dozen magazines in England that focus entirely on clay-target shooting or print several articles per issue on the sport. Most of the ink in British shooting magazines is aimed at sporting clays.

The booming interest in sporting clays in the United States has generated the first publication dedicated primarily to sporting clays, *Sporting Clays Magazine*. This magazine is also the official publication of The National Sporting Clays Association. *Shotgun Sports Magazine* is the official publication of the United States Sporting Clays Association and runs a regular sporting clays department every month with additional features on the sport. *Outdoor Life* runs a monthly sporting clays column

1

Sporting clays offers the shotgunner year-round shotgunning fun.

Sporting Clays: A Description of the Game

and provides a trophy to the winner of sporting clays national tournaments. Bob Brister began covering sporting clays in *Field & Stream* back in 1980 and writes frequent articles on the sport in his column.

Just as for trap and skeet shooting, it is hard to estimate exactly how many people shoot sporting clays for fun. Memberships in sporting clays associations and participants in tournaments are trends that can be accurately measured and these indicators reflect remarkable enthusiasm for the sport.

It is easy to understand why sporting clays has such universal appeal for enthusiasts who love shotguns and shooting. Sporting clays offers the shotgunner a multitude of recreational and competitive options. The shooter can participate as a serious competitor in local, state, regional, national, and international tournaments. He may be just an occasional tournament shooter several times a year, or he may abandon his couch-potato status and actively participate in competition on a regular basis. He may participate to improve his wingshooting skills or use sporting clays to provide year-round shooting when hunting seasons are closed.

Sporting clays provides an opportunity for shooters to earn national and international recognition. Bobby Jernigan (shooting) and Gale Davis (far left) both competed on the USA team at the World Sporting Clays Championships in England.

Some major corporations are choosing sporting clays as an alternative to golf for client entertainment or employee social events. Many companies sponsor teams in local sporting clays leagues. When I was at the Rocky Comfort Course in Quincy, Florida, I was told they had more shooters coming from one company in a single day than the total number of shooters during their entire first year of operation. The list of reasons why so many people are trying sporting clays goes on and on. I think the sport's tremendous growth in this country is due to one simple factor—it is just about the most fun you can have with a shotgun!

A sporting clays layout is called a *course*, which consists of several *fields*. These fields are usually named after the type of game-shot they simulate, such as "Driven Grouse," "Woodcock Alley," "Decoying Mallards," and "Flushing Quail." The naming of these fields often gets

Many corporations are choosing sporting clays as an alternative to golf for client and employee social functions.

Some fields feature rolling targets that duplicate the unpredictable antics
of bolting rabbits.

rather creative, producing such titles as "Kamikaze Grouse" and "Dirty
Ducks." On each field there may be several shooting positions that are
called *stands, stations,* or *butts.* A field may have one or more traps.

The trap operator is usually called a *trapper.* Many shooters will call
out "Trapper ready?" prior to calling for a target. This is a good idea
when one trapper is operating more than one trap at a time.

A variety of targets and target presentations are the major differences
between sporting clays and either trap or skeet. This is evident in the
courses themselves. No two are alike. *Forbes* magazine has called sport-

5

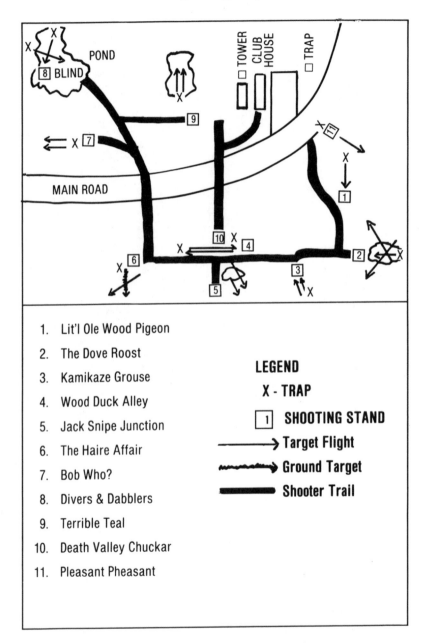

1. Lit'l Ole Wood Pigeon
2. The Dove Roost
3. Kamikaze Grouse
4. Wood Duck Alley
5. Jack Snipe Junction
6. The Haire Affair
7. Bob Who?
8. Divers & Dabblers
9. Terrible Teal
10. Death Valley Chuckar
11. Pleasant Pheasant

LEGEND

X - TRAP

1 **SHOOTING STAND**

⟶ **Target Flight**

⟶ **Ground Target**

━━ **Shooter Trail**

A typical sporting clays facility, showing the various stations.

Heartbreak Ridge
1107 8th Avenue
Albany, GA 31707

INVOICE #

For Reservations: 912-435-1555

Lodge: 912-787-5032

SPORTING CLAYS

FIELD	# TARGETS															TOTAL	REFEREE
1																	
2																	
3																	
4																	
5																	
6																	
7																	
8																	
9																	
10																	
11																	
12																	

TOTAL SCORE _____

NAME _____

ADDRESS _____

_____

USSCA # _____   COMPETITOR # _____   CLASS _____

A typical scorecard.

ing clays "golf with a shotgun." The very nature of a sporting clays course is conducive to easy change so that shooters do not get bored shooting the same old targets every time they visit the course. There are several ways to offer shooters new and challenging shots and keep the course fresh. It is a simple matter of moving a trap, moving a shooting station, or merely taking a few turns on the trap spring. Do any one of the three and it is a whole new target. Smart gun-club managers have realized this and change courses frequently to provide new challenges and opportunities for shooters to improve shotgunning skills.

A sporting clays field usually duplicates the types of shots offered by various game birds or animals. Even though the actual flight of the targets will differ, it simulates general behavior patterns of game species such as grouse, quail, pheasant, dove, pigeon, snipe, woodcock, waterfowl, and even rabbit. This variety of game duplication allows the shooter to experience shooting at various species of game that are not native to his part of the country. The south Georgia quail hunter can enjoy targets that mimic those offered to a South Dakota pheasant hunter without ever leaving home. Sporting clays also provides the opportunity to a hunter who is planning a trip for exotic game he has never

Some sporting clays fields such as this one, which resembles a Scottish moor and features incoming targets that mimic driven grouse, have an international flavor.

Sporting clays provides shooters with an opportunity to practice and hone skills on difficult shots like this high-crossing target that duplicates doves flying overhead.

hunted before to practice on targets that simulate that species. If you plan a trip to Scotland to shoot driven grouse, you can probably locate a sporting clays course nearby that has a driven-grouse field. Several afternoons shooting incoming targets duplicating driven grouse will do wonders for your score on these unusual targets. Not only will it make you look good, you will also elevate the reputation of other Yanks who cannot afford to shoot grouse in Scotland.

This duplication of game-bird species affords the hunter just about the best opportunity available to become an outstanding game shot. Modern bag limits do not provide enough shooting experience for hunters to approach their optimum shooting ability. You can shoot more springing teal, decoying mallards, or settling woodies in one afternoon on a sporting clays course than you can legally shoot in a whole season of duck hunting.

Another advantage to using sporting clays to improve your success on live game is that you can shoot the same type of target over and over. If you are having trouble with pass shooting, hitting decoying ducks or high doves, just go to the field that simulates these problem shots and practice until you reach the desired level of proficiency.

Participation in sporting clays tournaments is growing faster than any other competitive shooting sport in America. There are two basic organizational formats for shooting sporting clays tournaments: European rotation and squad rotation. European rotation allows the shooter to select the fields and shoot them in any order he wishes within a given time frame. Squad rotation is a round-robin affair in which the shooters are assigned to a squad and report to various stations in sequence and at an assigned time.

When shooting sporting clays, the shooter will be located on a shooting stand with well-defined boundaries. This stand usually includes one or more barriers that prevent him from accidentally swinging his gun toward other waiting shooters or spectators. He will load only at the referee's command to do so. Only two shells can be loaded at a time. When the shooter is loaded and ready to shoot, he calls for the target. Unlike American skeet and trap, the target may not be released immediately, but after a delay of up to three seconds.

The shooter must keep the gun off the shoulder and clearly visible under the armpit until the target is visible. This requirement allows for a more realistic duplication of field-shooting conditions than does the traditional mounted-gun position used by American trap and skeet shooters. This low-gun position is not as exaggerated as the "gun butt touching the hip" position used in international trap and skeet games for Olympic competition.

Some courses include a "walk-up" field that simulates the quail-walk format that enjoyed a modicum of popularity several years ago. This walk is usually about ten yards long with the targets released at the discretion of the referee. The shooter must reload between pairs of targets within a specified period of time, usually about five seconds. Occa-

Flushing-quail fields help bird hunters sharpen their skills for the season opener.

sionally, this field will feature a covey rise to test the shooter's ability to focus in on specific targets and hit them. Scoring may vary on the covey rise. Some shoot managers will allow multiple kills with one shot, others allow only one kill per shot. Another variation allows multiple kills on a single shot, but a maximum of only two kills per covey rise.

Fields offering long crossing shots are often called *pigeons* in England and frequently *passing ducks* in the United States. These targets are particularly nasty and can be extremely intimidating for the new shooter when thrown from a high tower. There is a consolation, however: a lot of shooters miss, so embarrassment is equally shared by all.

Springing-teal targets are launched straight up and offer shots very similar to jump-shooting ducks.

Driven grouse come toward the
shooter flying hard and fast.

"Springing teal" targets simulate jump-shooting puddle ducks. These
are usually thrown as simultaneous pairs and fly almost straight up. The
degree of difficulty increases with distance.

"Driven grouse" fields are designed to mimic shots offered by driven
grouse in Scotland, England, and Europe. These fast-traveling, low incoming shots are often launched from behind a low hill, tree line, or
thicket. Some clubs have even constructed realistic stone grouse butts to
add a little additional flavor to these fields.

"Flushed grouse" are outgoing targets that quarter away from the station at various ranges. These may be fairly close or rather long shots

13

Driven pheasant fields feature high, fast-flying incoming targets.

that have begun to settle back to earth at the end of their flights.

"Rabbit" targets are rolled rather than thrown. The clay target man-ufactured just for this field is about the same diameter as standard clay targets but has a thick rim that allows it to roll and bounce along the ground. Just like its real-life counterpart, this clay bunny is capable of unpredictable hops and bounces. This station may also feature a hay bale or other obstacle to offer the target sanctuary at the end of its run. This rabbit target is often combined with an aerial target and entitled "fur and feather," "fur and fowl," or "rat and bat."

In addition to allowing opportunities for multiple choices in target pre-sentation, sporting clays targets themselves come in a variety of shapes, sizes, and colors. The most common target thrown is the standard trap and skeet target. Targets for international skeet and trap are popular with many clubs because of their durability; they are designed to be thrown at higher speeds than conventional trap and skeet targets. The rather extensive list of targets includes midis, minis, battue, rockets, poi-son or hen, and others. These specific targets will be discussed in detail in a later chapter.

The "high pheasant" or "driven pheasant" duplicates high incoming targets. It gets its name from the driven-pheasant style of British shoot-ing in which beaters flush the birds over waiting hunters. If you can hit high passing doves or geese over white spreads, then you will do better than most on this stand.

Some stations are just plain devious. I remember one field I encoun-tered in my first exposure to sporting clays at the 1987 National Sport-ing Clays Championships, which was held in conjunction with the World Skeet Shooting Championships, in San Antonio. This was a report pair with the first target a ninety-degree right to left crossing shot that was going at what appeared to be twice the speed of sound. This target was rather low and never got above the background vegetation. You had to shoot this first target very, very fast. The second target came from the shooter's left over the top of a very thick oak tree and fell straight down once it cleared the tree. It appeared to be as big as a garbage-can lid and hovering motionless in the sky. This station was what my college foot-ball coach would have called a "character builder."

Targets may be thrown as singles, a true or simultaneous pair, a following pair, or report pair. A true pair or simultaneous pair is when two targets are launched at the same time. A following pair is two targets launched one right behind the other. In a report pair, the second target is released at the sound of the shot being fired at the first target.

Unlike trap and skeet shooting, you don't have to break 100 straight to be competitive. On a well-designed course the very best shooters will break scores in the mid or high 80s, with over half the shooters breaking more than 50 percent of their targets.

The hunter or shooter who is just taking up trap or skeet sooner or later gets on a squad of experienced competitors who crush or smoke nearly every target they shoot at. It is not much fun to hit only 75 out of 100 when you are shooting with others who are breaking 99s and 100s. In sporting clays everyone misses; there is not nearly the embarrassment experienced by beginners in other clay-target sports.

If you have become bored with other clay-target games or your enthusiasm for hunting is on the wane, you owe it to yourself to try sporting clays. Even if you are already an active clay-target shooter and avid hunter, sporting clays will broaden your shotgunning horizons and increase your opportunity to use your favorite "gravel squirter" on a year-round basis.

2
HOW TO GET STARTED

•

In England, most of the sporting clays winners are using over-and-unders from Beretta, Browning, and Winchester. The only 100 straight I know about as this is being written was shot by a British mailman with a Remington 1100 field gun. Beretta and Remington autoloaders are popular because of their reduced recoil. These are especially popular with women and those shooters who are recoil-sensitive. Andy Banks, of Pearland, Texas, won the 1985 Sporting Clays National Championships with a Browning A-5. Jim Juhl, of Katy, Texas, won the 1986 Sporting Clays Championships with a Browning Citori High Post Skeet gun.

Many field guns used to hunt upland game are quite suitable for shooting sporting clays. The most common gun in the United States is the over-and-under, weighing seven and one-half or eight pounds with 28- or 30-inch barrels and interchangeable choke tubes.

As a general rule, the stocks on sporting clays guns do not have quite as much drop as American field guns. Sporting stocks usually have a shorter length of pull than is found on most field guns. The slightly higher stock reduces recoil and allows the shooter to view clay targets a little better without lifting his head off the stock. This higher stock will also result in a little higher point of impact. The shorter length of pull allows the gun to be mounted a little faster with less chance of the recoil pad dragging or getting hung up in the shooter's clothing.

Many shooters use the same gun they hunt with to shoot sporting clays. Next to over-and-unders, autoloaders are the most popular.

The drop on your field-gun stock can be raised by adding a cheek pad or spacer to the comb of the stock. Several companies produce these devices, which are attached to your stock with velcro or adhesive backing. These spacers are an inexpensive way to modify your gun to shoot a little higher.

It is rather ironic that if you take a 30-inch over-and-under trap gun, put screw in chokes in it, and add a skeet stock, you would have a gun that comes pretty close to the specifications on sporting clays guns now being offered by many manufacturers. The popularity of sporting clays on this side of the Atlantic has generated considerable competition

Most serious competitors use over-and-unders with screw-in tubes.

among firearms manufacturers to meet the demands for "sporting clays guns." Beretta, Winchester, Classic Doubles International, and Browning have been manufacturing sporting clays guns for the British market for many years and are now promoting their guns in the U.S.

As this is being written, Browning is offering no less than eight sporting clays models. Beretta has six models for the sporting clays shooter. Perazzi has the MX-3 Sporting and the Perazzi Sporting Classic. Krieghoff offers multiple choices in options for the K-80 enthusiast who wants to mix and match a sporting clays gun. Winchester made the Model 550 for the European sporting clays market, and those turn up on this side of the Atlantic occasionally.

Many beginning sporting clays shooters are simply using field-grade

19

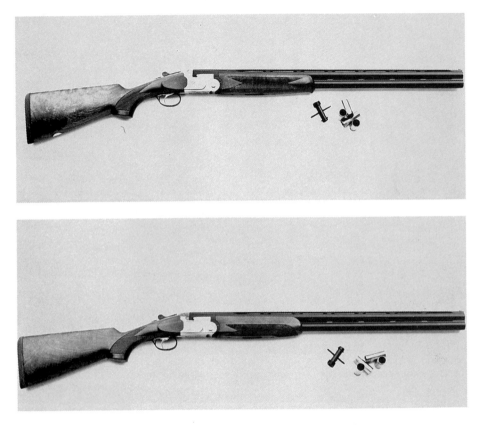

Beretta makes several special sporting clays models—like these 687L Sporting and 682 Sporting, both 12-gauge.

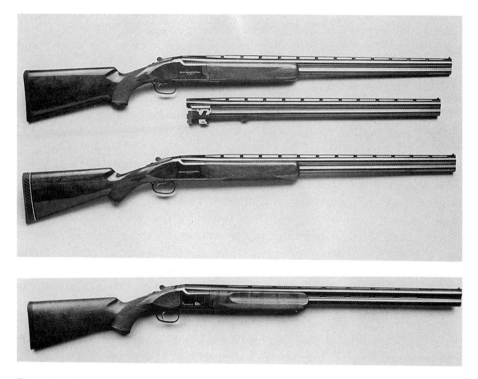

Browning also makes several guns that are designed especially for
sporting clays.

over-and-unders with screw-in choke tubes. A lot of Browning Lightning Citoris and Ruger Red Labels show up at sporting clays courses. If you get a Ruger Red Label, you may want to ship it back to the factory and have them convert the automatic safety to a manual safety.

A fair percentage of the serious sporting clays competitors are having their over-and-under barrels ported to reduce muzzle jump and recoil. This can be a considerable advantage when shooting simultaneous pairs.

Don't rule out the gas guns as sporting clays choices. The Remington 1100, 11-87, and Beretta 303 all see a lot of use by some respectable shooters. The major disadvantage I see with any single-barrel gun is the lack of a different choke in a second barrel for those fields where the targets in a pair are at various distances. This is only a minor disadvantage, but one that may present itself several times when shooting a 100-target course. I know one outstanding shooter, Chappie Gennett, winner of the 1989 Southeastern Shotgun Championships—which included registered sporting clays and skeet and trap events—who carried extra barrels for his Remington 1100 around from station to station on the sporting clays portion of that competition.

As your enthusiasm and addiction to sporting clays grows, you may want to add additional gear, such as a shell bag, an over-and-under shotgun designed for sporting clays, a competition vest, and other goodies. Don't feel you have to have a "sporting clays special" with fancy engraving and gold pheasant inlays to get started in the game. A large percentage of American shooters are shooting field-grade guns and wearing camo hunting vests.

If you are an upland-game hunter, you probably have everything you need to shoot sporting clays immediately. An open-choked field gun, a hunting vest, and a supply of shells loaded with 1⅛ ounces of number 8 shot is all you need for starters. Be sure to acquire shooting glasses and ear protection before shooting any clay-target sport.

Shooting glasses are a must when shooting clays. Many targets are incomers and you may get showered with target fragments. I have been hit twice by clay fragments that were big enough and moving fast enough to cut my skin. Either fragment would have done serious damage to an unprotected eye. Shooting glasses are also an IQ test of sorts. Sporting clays shooters who don't wear them probably have an IQ down around the level of plant life.

How to Get Started

Shooting glasses with interchangeable lenses have another advantage in addition to eye protection. As you learn more about shooting sporting clays, you will realize the important relationship between seeing targets and hitting them. A set of modern shooting glasses with several inter-changeable lenses will allow you to see targets better in difficult lighting conditions.

If you only plan to shoot sporting clays to improve your wingshooting skills, I suggest you not wait until just a few weeks before the season opener. If one or two trips to a sporting clays course just before the season opener helps a little, imagine how much better your skills will be if you shoot several times each month on a year-round basis. Why let your shotgun sit idle in the closet while your eye-hand coordination rusts for nine months out of the year when you could be improving your shooting skills and having fun doing it?

Many sporting clays facilities have resident instructors available, or may have someone like Jon Kruger or Jim Carlisle coming in to teach a seminar or provide several days of instruction. I strongly urge you to

World-class shooter Holly Haggard is also a highly qualified instructor since she has taken lessons from many top instructors on both sides of the Atlantic.

King Howington is one of the outstanding sporting clays shooters in the
United States and a serious student of the game who constantly searches
for better ways to break targets. He also has a well-deserved reputation
as an excellent instructor.

take advantage of instruction whenever it is available. Most of the top
competitive shooters got to their high level of ability by taking lessons
from many qualified instructors. A good shooting instructor is the best
way to make a lot of progress in the shortest possible time. If your goal
is to improve wingshooting skills for next hunting season or to be a competitive shooter, a shooting instructor is the way to go.

Because sporting clays is a relatively new sport in this country and
good shooting instructors come and go, I would be glad to send suggestions on selecting instructors from the current crop if you will send a
self-addressed stamped envelope to: Jerry Meyer, Route 1, Box 309,
Talking Rock, Georgia 30175.

Sporting clays provides an ideal training environment for the young
shooter. Most youngsters dream of the time they can finally accompany
adults on a hunt for quail, ducks, or doves. Their enjoyment of these

24

first few hunts can be dampened considerably if they shoot poorly. The ego and confidence often suffer. Several trips to a sporting clays course will go a long way toward making a youngster's first hunting trip a memorable one. It also provides a training experience for beginning shooters to reinforce safe gun-handling techniques.

When shooting sporting clays, always keep the action open on autoloaders and pumps. Doubles should be kept broken open at all times, except when you are on station and ready to shoot. It is better to be safe than embarrassed when another shooter has to caution you about unsafe gun-handling practices.

Most shooters like to watch several other people shoot a station before they try it. This gives them a chance to observe and decide how they want to shoot the station. Observers often get into conversation with friends and squad-mates on what the targets are doing and the best way to attempt breaking them. As a matter of simple courtesy, keep conversations down to the whisper level when another shooter is on station and calling for targets.

I am often surprised at the number of sporting clays shooters who have never hunted, or who used to hunt but have either stopped or slacked off considerably. Many "burned out" trap and skeet shooters are finding considerable enthusiasm for the sport.

Because the number of sporting clays courses increases daily, any attempt to include a list of places to shoot would be futile. I suggest you contact either of the following for a list of sporting clays courses:

> National Sporting Clays Association (NSCA)
> P.O. Box 680007
> San Antonio, Texas 78268

> United States Sporting Clays Association (USSCA)
> 50 Briar Hollow
> Suite 490 East
> Houston, Texas 77027

Finding the nearest course may be as simple as asking your local sporting goods or firearms dealer where to shoot sporting clays. It shouldn't be hard to find one closeby because new courses are springing up almost daily.

I frequently find myself having to spend a weekend out of town on business trips, so I always try to locate a nearby sporting clays course where I can spend some time shooting. It sure beats sitting in a motel room and watching cable TV all weekend.

3
KNOW YOUR GUN

•

Trap and skeet shooters have a pretty good idea about the distances of the targets they will be shooting. Skeet shooters will take all their targets fairly close, from 10 to 25 yards. Trap shooters will be shooting targets at longer distances, from 30 to 45 yards. A sporting clays shooter will have chances at targets that may be no more than 10 or 15 yards away, up to longer shots that may be 45 or 50 yards away. Therefore, a sporting clays shooter must be familiar with his gun's performance over a wider range of distances.

You will probably learn more about what your shotgun will do at various ranges when shooting sporting clays than in any other type of shooting. The relationship of chokes, shot size, shot hardness, pattern size, and pattern density to shotgun performance will become obvious after you shoot a few rounds of sporting clays.

Chokes

I do not think I will ever buy another shotgun without interchangeable choke tubes. I certainly would not choose a sporting clays gun without interchangeable tubes. The advantages of interchangeable choke tubes greatly outweigh the difference in purchase price of the gun.

Choke is a relative term. Several factors may influence the actual pattern density and diameter from a specific choke. A partial list of these factors would include brand of shell, size of shot, dram-equivalent, hardness of shot, burning rate of the powder, shot-load pellet-protector cup, or absence of a shot-load pellet-protection cup. Obviously, the amount of constriction between the bore diameter and choke diameter has a major impact on pattern characteristics.

AMERICAN CHOKE TERMINOLOGY

Percentage of Shot Pellets in a 30-Inch Circle at 40 Yards

CHOKE	PERCENTAGES
Extra Full	80 and Over
Full	70–80
Improved Modified	65–70
Modified	55–65
Improved Cylinder	45–55
Skeet (30-inch circle at 25 yards)	50
Cylinder	45 and Under

BRITISH CHOKE TERMINOLOGY

CHOKE	PERCENTAGES
Full	70 and Over
Three-Quarters	65–75
Half	60–65
Quarter	55–60
Improved Cylinder	45–55
True Cylinder	45 and Under

The point system of designating choke is based upon the concept of relative constriction, or difference between the actual diameter of the bore and the choke constriction. Each point of choke equals a constriction of 1/1000 of an inch (.001). A choke with 40 points of constriction is simply a choke that is 40/1000 (.040) smaller than the bore of the gun. Such a choke would be considered a Full Choke.

Know Your Gun

POINT SYSTEM TERMINOLOGY

POINTS	CHOKE
40	Full
30	Improved Modified
20	Modified
10 ✓	✓ Improved Cylinder
5	Skeet
0	Cylinder

The most practical choke for most sporting clays stations, if you could only choose one, is probably improved cylinder. In England the most common choke preference is what they call quarter choke, which throws a pattern only slightly tighter than American improved cylinder. Although improved cylinder is the best compromise for a single choke, it is not the best choke for all sporting clays targets. There are still many stations upon which a choke other than improved cylinder would provide some advantage.

One specific example comes to mind. I once encountered a fur and feather station on the Pigeon Mountain Course that screamed for cylinder choke. This station was in a narrow ravine with a bolting rabbit running left to right followed by a flushing grouse also crossing left to right on report. Both targets were no more than 20 yards away. The first time I shot this difficult pair I was shooting 3-dram 8s through improved cylinder choke tubes. On my next visit to that station I shot Federal Gold Medal Lites with number 9 shot through a cylinder choke and my score showed a substantial improvement.

I gained several advantages with this choke and load change. The Lite load reduced recoil, allowing for a quicker recovery for the report grouse target (this advantage would be even greater when shooting a simultaneous pair). Going to a smaller shot size put more pellets in the air and the cylinder choke gave me a larger pattern at this close range.

Another occasion where I chose cylinder choke and skeet loads with number 9 shot for a close rabbit target was at the 1989 USSCA National Championships at Game Hill Hunting Club in Weston, Missouri, where rabbit targets were thrown as simultaneous doubles! Many sporting clays shooters chose 7½s for rabbit targets because the target is thick and heavy enough to withstand numerous impacts with the ground. They don't believe number 9 shot will break these heavy-duty targets. My second pair of rabbits at this tournament disproved this theory.

These double rabbits usually split up right out of the traps, and as one is bouncing up, the other is falling or just rolling along the ground. It is difficult for most shooters just to look at one target and focus on breaking it. When my second pair came out, I picked a target and shot at it. Just as I pulled the trigger, I looked for my second target and didn't see it. I thought the second one had broken in the trap or had not been thrown. Then to my surprise the referee called "Dead and dead." In a state of total confusion I turned and looked back at Sue King who was standing just behind me, and she said, "The second target was directly behind the one you shot at. You smoked them both!" When I finished the station several shooters asked me what load I was shooting that would smoke one rabbit target and a second one right behind it. Very few of them believed me when I told them Winchester Super-Lite Skeet shells with number 9 shot. I even heard one shooter mumble something about seeing a small mushroom-shaped cloud exit my muzzle when I fired.

Both of these incidents occurred early in my sporting clays career, and because I shot competitive skeet for several years, I know the value of open chokes and small shot at close range. This confidence in open chokes and small shot cost me some targets at longer ranges when I first started shooting sporting clays. The more open chokes such as cylinder and skeet do offer advantages when a target must be taken at close range or when passing overhead. They are ideal for those occasional stations where the bird will almost land on you if you miss it. Some doubles require that one of the pair be taken at very close range, here a cylinder or skeet choke would offer some advantage on these close targets.

Another field requiring cylinder chokes and number 9 shot was the Prairie Chicken Field at the 1989 USSCA National Championships. This was an incoming simultaneous pair that came over the crest of a hill and passed directly over the shooter's head. The shooter was down in a pit blind that was about four feet deep. The targets were probably no more than 10 to 15 yards away as they passed over the shooter's head. This pair of targets was moving so fast that many shooters only got off five or six shots on the ten targets thrown. It was very similar to shooting simultaneous pairs from a pit blind on a skeet low house from station 8!

If you spend a little time patterning your gun with number 9 skeet loads through cylinder chokes at 20 yards, you will discover that the cylinder pattern is about 10 percent larger than improved cylinder at the same yardage in most guns. I am willing to change chokes for that percentage of improvement in effective pattern diameter. When I first started shooting sporting clays, my scores on close targets, rabbits, and overhead targets was considerably higher than other types of targets. I con ribute this early success on these close targets directly to cylinder choke and number 9 skeet loads.

Don't take my word for the effectiveness of number 9 skeet loads and cylinder chokes on any clay targets out to 25 yards. Spend some time testing your gun on a pattern board or simply place a few clay targets at this range and observe the consistency with which they are destroyed.

The only way to be absolutely sure what degree of choke you are getting from a specific load in your gun is to fire a few test patterns. I know shooters who spend thousands of dollars for guns, hundreds on lessons, and shoot thousands of shells in practice, but never take a few afternoons to test shot patterns. The most common procedure for evaluating chokes and the patterns they produce is firing a load into a thirty-inch circle on a piece of paper at a distance of 40 yards, counting the number of shot holes within that circle, and then dividing that number by the total number of shot pellets in the load to get a percentage. All this testing proves is whether or not your gun and choke combination is producing a pattern that matches the manufacturer's designation on the barrel or choke tube.

Rather than count all those hundreds of pellet holes and figure all those percentages, you may want to take various targets and hold them up to a pattern sheet to evaluate the effectiveness of that specific choke and shot size at various distances. You can make Plexiglas templates for the various targets—such as standard, midi, battue, and mini—to simplify this method of checking gaps in various combinations of shot size, choke, and distance.

Comparing the actual targets to pattern-test paper that has been shot at different ranges will give you some pretty accurate indications about

31

pattern density for specific load, shot size, and choke combinations. Just hold the different sporting-clays targets or Plexiglas templates up to the paper to see how many gaps there are in a pattern for that particular target. It takes several shots with each load and choke combination to get an accurate indication of pattern performance. Pattern testing is a game of averages. One or two shots at a pattern sheet will not provide the reliable comparisons you seek.

Don't evaluate patterns just for pattern diameter and shot density. Check for point of impact. Does your gun print a higher percentage of shot above or below the aim point? Does it shoot left or right? Do both barrels of your over-and-under shoot to the same place?

To test your gun for point of impact, draw a four-inch aiming spot in the center of a large sheet of paper (thirty-six to forty inches) and shoot at it from about 25 yards. Then examine the pattern to see if it printed

The only way to be sure that your gun is shooting where you are looking is to conduct a few pattern impact tests.

high, low, left, or right. It usually takes three to five shots on the same sheet of paper to achieve an accurate evaluation of point of impact. If you shoot a double barrel, you need to test point of impact for each barrel. Do not be overly concerned if your gun prints its patterns a little high. Most guns are set up to shoot just a little high. This allows you to see the target just above the rib rather than having to point directly at the target and partially obscure it.

I strongly recommend you test several combinations of chokes, shot sizes, and loads to determine which combinations are best in your specific gun. Just as a rifle may shoot tighter groups with a specific load and two identical automobiles require a slightly different carburetor adjustment, your shotgun will perform different from any other. The only way to know for sure how a load, shot size, and choke combination performs in your specific firearm is to test them in your gun.

I realize that many readers will not take the time to do extensive pattern testing with various loads and chokes; here are "quickie" alternatives. To check point of impact, place clay targets on a dirt bank about 15 yards away and shoot at them to check point of impact. Have an observer tell you if the pattern is centering the targets or hitting high, low left, or right. It is difficult to observe shot impact yourself, you may blink and not be able to evaluate pattern impact around the target accurately.

Pattern efficiency can also be evaluated by placing targets on a dirt bank and shooting at them from several yardages, using various combinations of loads and chokes. Neither of these techniques is recommended as a substitute for intensive testing of pattern performance in your gun. Both of these "quickie tests" are just that—a quick way to get some general ideas about your gun's performance. These tests will probably only identify major problems. I strongly encourage more intensive tests when time permits.

Chokes, loads, and patterns for sporting-clays shooting will be covered in detail in Chapter 6. I recommend *Shotgunning: The Art and the Science* by Bob Brister if you would like to learn more about shotgun-pattern efficiency on upland game birds and waterfowl.

4

BASIC SHOOTING TECHNIQUES

•

Basic Gun-Handling Skills

Your success with a shotgun will be in direct proportion to your mastery of basic fundamentals. Long before a sporting clays shooter begins to master the specific techniques for various types of target presentation (such as rabbits, overhead, quartering away, and others), he or she must master a few component skills necessary for consistency and accuracy.

Failure to master correct foot positioning, reading targets, gun-mount, swing, and follow-through will prevent a shooter from ever coming anywhere near optimum personal skill development. Lack of attention to any one of these skills will result in something less than peak performance on a sporting clays course or while hunting game birds in the field.

Foot Position

There are various methods for establishing correct foot position, and you need to determine which works best for you. Competitive trap and skeet shooters have long recognized the importance of foot position. If your feet are not placed properly, you will eliminate your ability to track the target visually, swing your gun, and follow through. Failure to position your feet correctly greatly reduces your chances of hitting the target before it is ever launched.

Your feet must be positioned to allow your upper body to continue pivoting as you swing the gun past the location where you expect to break the target. Many beginning shooters position their feet toward the eye's focal point and too close to the trap machine, rather than setting up in a position that allows them to swing past the point where they expect to break the target.

There are several methods for determining how to place your feet. One method that works for many people is simply to point the front foot directly toward the spot you expect to break the target. Some shooters prefer to mount the gun and actually swing past the expected target-breaking area to make sure they will be able to keep the gun moving past where they intend to break the target.

It is quite common to see shooters use a stance that is much too wide, especially when on unlevel ground. If your stance is too wide, your feet more than nine to eleven inches apart, this will greatly reduce your

Your front foot should point to the target break-point. This will always allow your body to continue pivoting during the follow-through after the shot is fired.

range of swing and ability to keep your shoulders level when swinging on crossing shots. If you doubt this, here is how you can find out for yourself. Stand with your feet shoulder-width or wider apart. Mount an empty gun and swing as far left and right as possible and use something to mark the maximum swing in each direction. Now place your feet about nine inches apart with the left foot pointing at twelve o'clock and slightly in front of your right, which is pointing at approximately two o'clock. Repeat the test for maximum left and right swing and measure the extremes. I rest my case.

Too wide a stance can also produce what is referred to as "rainbowing," or tipping the shoulders from a horizontal position when tracking crossing targets. Rainbowing is simply the dropping of the shoulder nearest the direction of rotation; if you are rotating right, the right shoulder drops. The longer you track a crossing target from too wide a stance, the more pronounced the rainbow effect. Occasionally there are sporting clays targets that are not crossing from left to right in a horizontal plane, and the shooter must deliberately cause his shoulders to dip below a level position in order to track the target. With a stance that is too wide, the rainbow effect is unintentional and uncontrollable.

If you have to tip your shoulders to track a target that is dropping rapidly in front of you, put your weight on your front foot with just the ball of your rear foot in contact with the ground, and you will be able to control upper-body position as you track and swing crossing targets falling rapidly in front of you. A good rule to follow is to keep your weight on the front foot for all those targets that are going away or falling in front of you. This is critical when attempting a target that has been launched from a position below you, such as the malicious chukar, which is usually launched from a bank or gully below the shooting station and begins to fall rapidly.

Reading Targets

Many people look at targets, but few see very much! Experienced shooters know there is much vital information to be gained by examining targets prior to stepping onto the station to shoot.

One of the first things you should learn on every station is where the target will first be visible after it is launched. I like to use some feature

36

such as a bush or limb to mark the spot where the target will appear. This will usually be my eye focal point, where I will pick up the target visually. If the target will be coming from a sharp angle, over your shoulder or even behind you, don't screw your body around or move your feet in order to see the target as soon as possible. Foot and body position should never be compromised just to see a target a little sooner. The target break-point should always be your top priority when positioning your feet and setting yourself up for a shot.

Once you have positioned yourself to break the target, then you can wind your upper body and turn your head back toward where the target will appear.

Since you won't be able to view the target from the station prior to shooting, the first target will look a little different from what you observed from behind the station. Even though you have located the spot where you think the target will first be visible, don't get "tunnel vision"; adjust your eyes for wide-angle vision.

If a target is launched at high speed, at a sharp angle, or very close to the shooter, it is often impossible to see anything but a blur. Trying to see one of these targets very early in its flight is difficult if not impossible. If there is a bad background, trying to see a target of this type when it is still a blur will often result in not being able to see the target at all and having it pass undetected. Minis are particularly hard to see clearly just after they are launched. My skeet-shooting coach, Dan Mitchell, once gave me some very good advice on when to visually pick up targets that were difficult to see due to a bad background. He suggested waiting until the target had traveled far enough to be seen clearly rather than trying to see it when it was right out of the trap and still nothing more than a blur.

There is much more to be learned from observing a target than just where it comes from and where it is going. Is it a standard, mini, midi, or battue? Is it rising or falling? Where in its flight is the trajectory most level? Where is target speed most uniform? Are there obstacles that will interfere with visibility or obstruct shot patterns? Is wind affecting target behavior? Does the sun become a factor at some time during the target's flight? Where in its flight will the target expose the largest surface area to your shot pattern?

Knowing which target is being thrown will help you in estimating speed and distance. Even experienced shooters often mistake a midi for a standard. It is an easy mistake to make. A midi often creates the illusion of being a standard target at a greater distance and traveling at a much faster speed. How can you determine if you are looking at a midi or standard? Just ask the trapper or referee what target is being thrown if you are not sure.

On some targets you may want to shoot quickly, before they become more difficult due to obstacles, wind effects, sharp dropping, or minimal surface-area presentation. Springing teal are good examples of targets that present many of the flight characteristics you should look for. They start off at high velocity right out of the trap, slow down to a stop at the peak of their flight, then begin to fall back down where they may be influenced by wind. If they are angling slightly away or are being blown by the wind, they may even turn edge-on and present a minimal target

Spend the time waiting by reading targets. Where is the target first visible? What is its line of flight? At what range do you expect to break it? Where is the target break-point? Where will your gun hold-point be? Where will your eye focal point be?

surface to be struck by shot pellets. Most good springing-teal shots will hit both targets on the way up, while trajectories and velocities are fairly constant.

All these factors need to be considered before you step onto the station to shoot. It is impossible to think about all these target characteristics while you are attempting to break a target. Prior observation is necessary for determining target break-points, eye focal points, and gun hold-points. This does not mean that you do not continue to respond to a target's behavior once you are on the station. But you will not have time to think and make decisions once the target is launched—you must react instinctively with your gun muzzles rather than think about what you must do. You have to look at a lot of sporting clays targets to develop the skills necessary to read them correctly. Reading targets is a talent you must constantly strive to improve.

There are three major decisions that must be made prior to stepping onto a station and attempting to break a target. First, you must decide on the general area in which you intend to break the target. This is what I call the *target break-point*. Once the target break-point is identified, you will then decide upon where the *eye focal point* and *gun hold-point* will be.

Target Break-Points

A target break-point is simply the approximate area in which you want to break the target. This is determined by carefully observing the target's flight characteristics prior to stepping onto the shooting station. Once you have determined the best location for the target break-point, then you will be able to correctly position your feet to break it and decide where your gun hold-point and eye-focus point will be. Several factors are important in selecting the target break-point. A few things to consider are natural barriers, distance to target, target flight, shot-pattern efficiency, and maximum exposure of target surface.

An example of taking advantage of maximum target surface area is the tower shot, or a target launched from behind you that passes directly over your head going directly away. If you shoot this target while it is directly, or nearly directly, over your head, then you have the entire bottom surface exposed to shot pellets. If you let it travel past you very

This shooter is visualizing where the target break-point will be prior to shifting his eyes back to the eye focal point and calling for the target.

far, then you will have a less desirable angle that only presents the thin target edge. Difficulty may be further increased by delaying too long the taking of this target and having to shoot it as it is dropping rapidly.

After you have established the target break-point, then you decide upon your eye focal point, where you will focus your eyes to pick up the target visually after it is launched. As a general rule, the longer you look at a target the better you are able to establish the target line and break it.

Somewhere between the target break-point and the eye focal point will be the gun hold-point, or the direction your muzzles will be pointing when you call for the target. There are no magic formulas or absolutes when it comes to deciding just how far these three positions should be separated from one another. Each shooter must determine through trial and error what the best combinations are for his or her particular style of shooting. But there are some general rules that will help get you into the ballpark.

I think most shooters would agree that you want to see the target as soon as possible in order to begin reading its line or flight path. Care must be exercised on those fields where there are bad backgrounds or minis are thrown. In either case, it is difficult to see anything but a blur just after a target is launched. You cannot read a target correctly until it has slowed down enough to be seen clearly. There is also a danger of failing entirely to see a fast target if your eye focal point is too close to the trap.

Gun Hold-Point

The gun hold-point is where you point your gun when you call for a target. On close fast-crossing targets, the gun hold-point is closer to the trap and the eye-focus point. On longer crossing targets or targets going almost directly away from you, the eye-focus point will be closer to the target break-point.

On crossing targets, the target should pass over the gun muzzles so that you will not lose sight of it. Be sure your muzzles are pointed under the expected target flight. Holding the muzzles above the target's path is a common mistake on targets with a relatively low trajectory.

It is also imperative to have a low gun hold-point on rabbit targets. Because rabbit targets are so unpredictable, you must be certain to hold your gun so that the rabbit is visible at all times. Many new shooters use a gun hold-point that is too high for this target because they fear the rabbit will bounce high in the air. On rabbit fields where the targets are close crossing shots, the gun hold-position should be very close to the eye-focus point.

Avoid tracking the target with the muzzles over a long distance because this tends to make most shooters too deliberate. When you get deliberate, the tendency is to "aim" your gun rather than "point" it. Tracking a target with the muzzles over a long distance will cause you to begin checking bead alignment and measuring lead. The result of both

41

Here King Howington demonstrates the correct low-gun position and gun hold-point as he waits for a right-to-left crossing target that will be launched low and to his right.

these practices will be an irregular and jerky swing, or a "dead gun" with no swing at all. Except on close crossing targets, which don't allow enough time to check and measure, the target hold-point should be fairly near the target break-point and positioned so that the target will pass the muzzles just before you mount your gun and fire.

The close, fast crossing at a right angle requires a gun hold-point close to the eye focal point. Distant targets crossing at a slight quartering angle, or those going directly away, require gun hold-points that are closer to the target break-point.

Eye Focal Point

The eye focal point is simply the location where you focus your eyes and first expect to see the target clearly. It is important to see the target as quickly as possible, but it is dangerous to look too close to the trap in low light or bad background situations. The human eye cannot see a clay target as anything but a blur when it has just been launched and is traveling over sixty miles an hour. Attempting to track any target with eyes or muzzles when it is still traveling too fast to be seen as anything but a blur is risky.

This shooter has selected his target break-point and his gun hold-point and has shifted his eyes back to the eye focal point prior to calling for the target.

All-America Sporting Clays shooter Gale Davis demonstrates his ready position with his gun stock below his armpit prior to calling for a target.

Observe the targets of other shooters as you are waiting for your turn in order to identify that point where the target ceases to be a blur and can be seen clearly. Minis are notoriously difficult to see when they first come out of the trap. Minis must be launched with considerable velocity because, due to their light weight, they lose velocity rapidly.

Avoid tunnel vision when looking at the eye focal point. Force yourself to hold your eyes on "wide-angle vision" until the target appears. Once you actually see the target at the eye focal point, then you must zero in on it with 100 percent visual and mental concentration.

44

Here Gale has completed his gun-mount after seeing the target. The gun is mounted by extending the right hand (Gale is left-handed) allowing the gun stock to rise up and make contact with his shoulder and cheek.

To further implement this shift from wide-angle vision as you wait to first see the target and to augment the total focus of mind and eye as you track and break the target, some shooters will focus on the front edge rather than the entire target.

Gun Mount

Many authorities agree that incorrect gun mounts contribute to more misses than any other single factor. To shoot moving targets with a shotgun, the gun must be pointed—not aimed. To clarify this concept, let me suggest an experiment. Select some rapidly moving object such as a passing car or a flying bird. Focus your eyes on the moving object, then quickly point your finger at the target while keeping your eyes focused on it. Now, while attempting to keep your finger pointed at the moving target, focus your eyes on your fingernail as you would on a shotgun bead when attempting to aim at a moving target. Now, focus back on the moving target and you will see that the finger is no longer aligned with the moving object; you probably will have fallen behind the target. The same thing will happen if you attempt to transfer your visual focus from a clay target to the bead and then back to the target. Your muzzles will invariably fall behind the target and you will shoot behind it.

Like most American shotgunners, I was self-taught through hunting game birds. I was in my late twenties before I ever shot at a clay target. I was in my midforties before I ever took a shooting lesson. My shooting skills improved more in one year after taking lessons than they did in the first thirty years I spent shooting game. Oh, I hit my share of quail, ducks, and doves, but I kept making the same mistakes over and over. My worst errors were committed in mounting my gun.

In the early days, whenever game was flushed, the very first thing I did was jam the butt of my gun against my shoulder and then jam my face down against the stock. Next, I looked at the bead so I could aim the shotgun. Then I started swinging toward my target and attempted to shoot out in front of the flying bird to a spot where I hoped the bird and shot would collide. A lot of them did—but a lot of them didn't.

After reading an article in an outdoor magazine on how to shoot doves, I began to swing through birds and "paint them out of the sky," as I called it. This swing-through method improved my ability to hit crossing targets considerably. But I was still separating gun-mount and the initiation of my swing, which contributed to a jerky stop-and-go motion. When I became addicted to sporting clays, I learned how to achieve maximum effectiveness by mounting my gun as my upper torso was swinging with the target. This is the system used by the great majority of the sporting clays shooters in England. After sixty years of shooting sporting clays, you have to believe the British have some pretty good ideas about how to play the game!

Avoid mounting the gun prematurely, before you have seen the target and accurately read distance, speed, and trajectory. There is a definite advantage in letting a shot "develop," slow down, and stabilize before attempting to shoot it. I do not like to allow a target to develop to the stage that it has begun to lose enough velocity to drop rapidly.

A good gun-mount begins with a good ready position, with the heel of the stock tucked under the armpit. Avoid holding the stock too low; it should be lightly touching your armpit. The stock only needs to extend up under your armpit for an inch or so. Your arm should be raised slightly to avoid clamping the stock up under your arm.

Some shooters like to hold the butt below the armpit, but rather than stick an inch or two of stock up under their armpit, they hold the butt in front without touching the body. I prefer the first method of placing an inch or two of stock under my armpit because it forces me to position the gun in exactly the same ready-position on every shot.

The gun is mounted by thrusting it forward with the left hand, if you are a right-handed shooter. The comb of the stock will come to rest against the cheek, but don't bring your head down to the stock. Your head shouldn't move. The shoulder is pushed forward or hunched slightly to make contact with the recoil pad.

Avoid the tendency to use the right hand to force the gun onto the shoulder. Apply only a gentle lifting pressure with the right hand.

As you are learning to mount your gun with this technique, make an effort to keep the barrels level. Avoid letting the gun pivot up and down on the left hand. This seesaw motion causes the muzzles to drop excessively as the gun is mounted, and will cause you to shoot low almost every time.

The gun-mount should never obstruct your vision of the target. Your gun hold-point and the gun itself should both be kept below the anticipated target flight path. This is why most guns are set up to shoot just a little high—so that targets are visible just above the rib when the barrels are correctly aligned with the target.

If you will practice this gun-mount (make sure the gun is empty) just twenty-five times a day for a week, you will see a noticeable improvement in your scores the next time you shoot. When practicing your gun-mount, don't look at the bead, instead focus your eyes on some distant object and point at it instinctively.

Don't worry about speed when practicing gun-mounts. Concentrate on the correct form. There is an old cliché that goes "Practice makes perfect." That is not true. Practice makes permanent. Only perfect practice makes perfect. Once the correct gun-mount is learned, the speed will come easily. In any case, you will always be able to mount the gun quicker than you will be able to read the correct line on a target.

Swing, Forward Allowance, and Gun-Mount

It is not uncommon to hear a new clay-target shooter ask a more experienced trap, skeet, or sporting clays shooter how much lead he is seeing on a specific target. Any answer should only be accepted as a ballpark figure, since many variables affect how much lead is seen by individual

Gun-mount, swing, forward allowance, and follow-through are all integrated motions and not separate moves to be performed individually—as demonstrated by Holly Haggard as she breaks the first sporting clays target ever thrown at Cherokee Rose Plantation.

shooters. A good shooting coach can watch you shoot, evaluate what is making you miss, and offer some suggestions on corrective measures. Only in rare circumstances can consistent problems on a specific type of sporting clays target be solved by simply seeing more or less lead. Lead or forward allowance results from several factors including foot position, gun-mount, reaction time of the shooter, hand speed, gun swing, visual skills, and the aggressiveness of the individual shooter.

The shooting style employed by a shooter will be of primary importance in determining how much lead he sees. A spot shooter who is not swinging his gun will require the longest lead of all. A sustained lead shooter will require more lead than a pull-ahead shooting style. The pass-through style of shooting requires the least lead of all. So, just asking someone how much he is leading a particular target will result in an answer that will probably be harmful rather than helpful.

There are several ways to cause a shot pattern and a moving clay target to collide. As in the old adage, "You have to hit 'em where they are—not where they were!" Lead or forward allowance may be acquired in several ways.

It is possible to spot-shoot a target. This method requires the shooter to anticipate where the target is going, estimate when it will arrive at a specific location, and precisely time the arrival of the shot pattern at that location. It can be done, and as I stated earlier, I used this system on wild game for many years. Then I learned the error of my ways. About the only time I spot-shoot a target now is on one of those occasions where I have visually lost a target or missed picking it up as it was launched and my only option was a last-ditch effort to poke the muzzles out front and break it. It is not a system any experienced shooter uses if there are other options. I must confess that any time I use this method now is a reflex response that reverts back to my use of this technique for so many years on wild game.

Sooner or later you will hear someone refer to the Churchill system of shooting. This system is based theoretically upon allowing the target to pass the muzzles before the gun is mounted, tracking the target with the eyes and upper body while the gun is still unmounted, then mounting the gun and firing as the muzzles point directly at the target with no apparent lead being seen by the shooter. The theory behind this system is that the rapid swing required to overtake the target at the last moment just before firing will provide the required lead to break the target.

Another method for obtaining the required lead is what many shooters call a "pull-ahead swing." This system requires the shooter to point the dismounted gun at the target, mount the gun while still pointing at the target, then pulling ahead, seeing the required amount of lead, and pulling the trigger.

Still another method is the "swing-through" method, which involves tracking the target with a dismounted gun, mounting the gun and pointing behind the target, and then swinging through the target and pulling the trigger when the appropriate lead is seen.

Many skeet shooters use a "sustained-lead method," in which the target is never allowed to pass the muzzles. The gun hold-point is far enough out in front of the target to allow the target to approach the muzzles of the moving gun until the correct lead is seen, and then with the gun still moving, the shot is fired.

Now, after having given these brief descriptions of the most common techniques for obtaining lead, I will tell you that most experienced sporting clays shooters use the combination of fast swing and shooting directly at close crossing targets. You must keep your gun moving to make this work for you. This same system is also popular for mid-range and quartering shots; again the key is to keep that gun moving.

When the subject of forward allowance for long crossing or quartering targets comes up, there is considerable difference of opinion whether any apparent lead should be seen by the shooter. I know some excellent shooters who swear by both systems. One of the major problem targets for me has been the long crossing or quartering-away shot. I can break targets with regularity out to 30 to 35 yards without seeing any apparent lead, but as distances increase, I have to see some space between the muzzles and the target. If I maintain a smooth swing and keep the gun moving as I see the correct lead, then I occasionally break the long ones. If I stop my swing as I check forward allowance, the target is always lost.

I do not mean to imply that you should focus on the bead of your gun when checking forward allowance. Lead on these long crossing shots should be obtained while focusing 100 percent on the target with the barrels out of focus and occupying your peripheral vision. Even those shooters who see some space between the muzzles and the target still use a swing-through or pull-ahead swing style. Very few sporting clays shooters use the sustained lead method to obtain forward allowance. The only time spot shooting is used is when it is an unintentional reversion to old bad habits.

I cannot, nor can anyone else, tell you how much lead to see on a sporting clays target. An experienced shooter, preferably a qualified instructor, can look over your shoulder and tell you if you are behind or in front of a target. There are no magic formulas. Once you have learned how to position your feet and mount and swing your gun, forward allowance will take care of itself.

The British advocate the concept of "swing and don't check" to emphasize the importance of trusting eye-hand coordination to point the muzzles and pull the trigger when everything is right to break a target. You can bet that major-league infielders are not estimating how many inches off the ground they have to hold their gloves to catch a ground ball. Quarterbacks do not mathematically calculate forward allowance in feet as a wide receiver is streaking toward the goal line. The real magic to the correct forward allowance is in first learning good shooting form and then practicing enough to program your own mental computer to know when to pull the trigger. If you doubt the validity of this concept, ask a good sporting clays shooter how much he leads a target and his first response will probably be a blank stare and then he might say something like, "I just shot right at it."

Even after you have worked with a good instructor and learned correct technique and have some concept of how much lead is required, you will need to practice until you subconsciously break targets without thinking about measuring the correct forward allowance. Usually if you have to think, you have already missed. Do your thinking before the target is in the air. Once it is launched, your brain should be on automatic pilot and locked onto the target.

Forward allowance is a difficult subject to address in specific terms for all the reasons I have mentioned. Beware the advisor who tells you exactly how far to lead all bolting rabbits, springing teal, or forty-yard crossers. He may not be intentionally giving you bad information, but what he sees and what you need to see will be different because it is impossible for two people to exactly duplicate each other's visual abilities, shooting style, eye-hand coordination, and mental acuity. Accept any such advice as an estimated guess at best.

You will often hear shooters refer to a smoke trail behind a target. Targets don't leave smoke trails, except in the minds of shooters. In an attempt to track a target and follow its true flight path with the muzzles, many shooters imagine the target is leaving a smoke trail and they actually visualize this trail and use it to guide their swing from behind and through the target. One of my regular sporting clays shooting partners, King Howington, is an excellent shot and shooting instructor who has distinguished himself in many major sporting clays tournaments. King visualizes an imaginary string attached to the target that he uses to track the target with his muzzles. All you have to do is look at his scores and you have to believe the concept has some merit.

Such mental devices are not just for experienced shooters. They also have considerable value for the new shooter who is having trouble reading a target's true flight path. Being able to read and follow with your muzzles the subtle little angles of target trajectories is a major factor in reaching your optimum personal potential in shooting sporting clays. A piece of imaginary string or a little smoke just might help.

Letting Yourself Go

Once you have learned the basic techniques and developed reasonably correct form by practicing on a regular basis, you are ready to make the final step in achieving your optimum personal performance. This final step is very simple to understand but difficult to implement: You must let yourself go. You must trust your subconscious mind when it tells you where to point the barrels and when to pull the trigger.

Like most other shooters, when I shoot poorly on a station, I get too deliberate. I become cautious, I check to see if everything is exactly right before I pull the trigger—and miss and miss and miss. On those days when I can't seem to miss, I feel very relaxed, I'm having fun and the targets seem to break as if by magic.

If I put a two-by-four on my living room floor and asked you to walk from one end to the other you could probably do so with ease. But if I suspended that same two-by-four between two ten-story buildings and then asked you to walk from one end to the other, I suspect the task would be considerably more difficult. The physical requirements of trav-

It's obvious in this photograph that world-class shooter Dave Bleha is about to "let himself go" as soon as this right-to-left crossing target is launched.

eling from one end to the other of both boards were the same; the difference in the degree of difficulty came when your conscious mind became involved. When we fear missing targets or feel pressure to shoot well in a big tournament, that same conscious mind takes over and everything gets to be deliberate—too deliberate! This tendency toward cautious deliberate action causes us to check leads, attempt to aim a shotgun instead of pointing it and swinging and trusting our natural eye-hand coordination.

Have you ever been on a dove field and seen a dove approaching from a long distance off? You wait patiently until he gets closer. You slowly raise your gun and take your time to check and make sure the lead is absolutely perfect, and then miss! You have probably also been sitting on a dove field and had a friend yell, "Hey! Over your head!"

53

You look up, and there, flying over your head and going like blazes, is a dove that approached you undetected. You mount your gun and reduce him to a puff of feathers. You didn't have time to calculate leads and check everything but barometric pressure, you pointed the gun and pulled the trigger when everything was right.

First comes learning good shooting form such as foot position, gun-mount, keeping your face on the stock, and a smooth swing. Once you have practiced these techniques, then you must learn to let yourself go so that the wondrous machine that is the human body can perform its miracles.

The Holland and Holland Sporting Clays videotape illustrates many of the shooting techniques I have described in this chapter. I urge all sporting clays shooters to get a copy.

5
SPORTING CLAYS TARGETS

•

The sporting clays shooter, unlike trap and skeet shooters, can expect to see a variety of targets when shooting a round. These targets will vary in size, shape, flight characteristics, and vulnerability to shot impact. The best hunters take the time to learn as much as they can about their quarry. Serious trap and skeet shooters know exactly what to expect from the targets they are required to shoot. To come anywhere near your own optimum skill level at sporting clays, you will need to be aware of the characteristics of each sporting clays target.

Many shooters are familiar with the standard clay target used in trap and skeet. It is possible to shoot a sporting clays course that will only consist of 70 percent standard targets. The remaining 30 percent will consist of the "specialty" targets such as minis, midis, battues, rabbits, and rockets. To better understand the differences between the standard and the other specialty targets, a description of the standard target is in order.

The Standard Target

The sporting clays standard target may be one that was manufactured for trap or skeet or it may be one of the new sporting clays targets with the same dimensions as those used for trap and skeet. The targets made

Some fields may feature a mix of targets such as a pair consisting of a standard and a midi. It's a good idea to be aware of this mixture prior to attempting to break them.

for sporting clays, however, will be slightly more durable. These targets are 4½ inches in diameter (108 mm) and about 1 inch high. Standard targets come in a variety of colors, including orange dome, yellow dome, all-black, all-orange, or all-white.

I have seen one field that consisted of a report pair with the first target being an all-orange standard followed by an all-black standard. These targets were launched in front of a wooded hillside background. Both traveled right to left at about a ninety-degree angle in front of the shooting station. Because it was much harder to see against the dark background, many shooters erroneously thought the black target was a smaller midi target or a standard traveling considerably faster than its orange predecessor. This mix of targets also contributed to another common mistake made by many shooters when they get a target that is difficult to see: They lift their heads off the stock in an effort to see the target better and the opportunity to shoot is missed. If you are ever in doubt about exactly which target is being thrown, don't be bashful—ask the trapper or referee.

If you are getting targets of different colors, try to see how far they are traveling. If they are both landing in approximately the same area, you will know they are traveling about the same speed. Knowing this will keep you from wrongly assuming the more visible target is traveling faster than the one that is harder to see.

Midi Targets

Midi targets are 3½ inches (90 mm) in diameter and ⅞ inch high. They are all-black or all-orange. These targets are frequently referred to by their metric measurement, "ninety millimeter." The two names for this target—midi and ninety millimeter—are used interchangeably all over the country.

Midis can be very deceptive and are often mistaken for what appears to be a larger standard target that is traveling faster at a greater distance. This is probably one of the most common optical illusions confronted by sporting clays shooters. This error can be especially easy to make if you are viewing targets out past 35 yards. It is not a bad idea to ask which targets are being thrown on all the longer targets just to make sure you are really seeing what you think you are seeing. As you will learn in Chapter 6, knowing the distance and type of target has considerable influence upon your selection of the correct choke and load combination.

You are in for a real experience the first time you see midis and standards thrown as a simultaneous pair from the same trap. The two targets will come out together and for a short time fly in fairly close formation. Then the midi will appear to streak ahead of the standard as if some sort of afterburner has been turned on. The midi has less wind resistance than the larger standard target, so it loses velocity less rapidly. Consequently, it appears to be speeding up. As with all simultaneous pairs, it is critical to select one target, focus on that selected target only, and break it before looking at the second target in the pair.

Another flight characteristic to look for when midis and standards are launched as a simultaneous pair is the considerable difference in the trajectory of the two targets. Since the standard loses velocity faster than does the midi, it will begin to drop earlier than the midi. The farther the pair travel, the more extreme the differences in velocity and rate of drop between them.

Chokes and Loads for Sporting Clays

Personally, I prefer to change chokes and loads to obtain optimum pattern performance. My car has a five-speed transmission; why should I drive around in one gear all the time? One of sporting clay's most appealing aspects is the variety of targets that duplicate various game birds. I don't hunt all game birds with the same choke and load, so why should I shoot sporting clays with only one choke and load?

Some shooters argue that they don't want to worry about whether or not they have the right choke in their gun when they are shooting. I don't either. That is why I look at the target on each field, make my choke/load decision and step up to shoot knowing I have the best possible choke/load combination for that specific target. If one choke and load were ideal for all shotgun targets, both clay and feathered, we shooters wouldn't buy different loads and guns with interchangeable chokes. If changing chokes only nets you one or two targets out of a hundred, it is worth the effort. I have driven home on numerous occasions as an "also shot" because some other shooter bumped me out of winning or placing in a tournament by one target.

Based upon nearly two thousand test firings at pattern paper and clay targets under controlled conditions, I have identified the following loads and chokes that produce optimum patterns in my specific gun-and-choke combinations. I have also included less-desirable choke/load combinations for comparison and the rationale for selecting the optimum choke/load at each distance.

Optimum Patterns

DISTANCE	LOAD	CHOKE	OPTIMUM PATTERN
15 yards	* Skeet 9	Cyl	20 inches
	Skeet 9	IC	17 inches
	Skeet 8	Cyl	17 inches
	Skeet 8	IC	10 inches

*This choice is obvious. The larger 20-inch optimum pattern is certainly an advantage for close work on those stations where targets are really close, such as fur and feather, woodcock, and driven grouse. Notice that this optimum load throws a pattern that is twice the size of improved cylinder 8s!

20 yards	* Skeet 9	Cyl	24 inches
	Skeet 9	IC	24 inches
	Skeet 8	Cyl	24 inches
	Skeet 8	IC	19 inches

*Optimum pattern diameters were nearly identical on three of these load/choke combinations. Cylinder 9s was selected as the best choice based on overall uniform pellet distribution plus more pellets in the middle (24.5-inch diameter) ring of the pattern. The other patterns had too large a percentage of pellets in the center (17.2-inch) ring.

25 yards	* Skeet 9	Cyl	30 inches
	Skeet 9	IC	30 inches
	Skeet 8	Cyl	26 inches
	Skeet 8	IC	24 inches

*Cylinder choke produced more uniform pellet distribution than did improved cylinder, with fewer gaps and more pellets dispersed in both the middle (24.5-inch diameter) and outer (30-inch diameter) portions of the pattern.

30 yards	* Skeet 9	Cyl	30 inches
	Skeet 9	IC	30 inches
	Skeet 8	Cyl	26 inches
	Skeet 8	IC	24 inches

*Higher pellet counts in the outer portion of the pattern was the deciding factor here. This is the maximum range at which number 9 pellets maintain sufficient energy to consistently fracture targets during my tests; consequently, they were not considered for loads at greater distances.

35 yards	* Trap 8	IC	30 inches
	Trap 7½	IC	20 inches
	Trap 8	Mod	20 inches

*Trap 8s in improved cylinder produced most uniform pellet distribution throughout the entire pattern and averaged ninety-six pellets in the outer ring. This pellet density of ninety-six (very close to the one-hundred-pellet minimum I have used in evaluating pellet density) in the outer ring of the pattern influenced me to chose trap 8s in improved cylinder. Modified choke and trap 8s produce denser pellet counts in the center (17.2-inch diameter) and middle (24.5-inch diameter) rings of the pattern and therefore might be a better choice for targets flying directly away or edge-on to the shooter and for shooting midis or minis. Trap singles are usually broken at a distance between 30 and 35 yards and many trap shooters shoot modified chokes and number 8 shot. This was another tough choice to make.

40 yards	Trap 8	IC	20 inches
	* Trap 8	Mod	24 inches
	Trap 7½	Full	24 inches

*Modified choke and trap 8s produced most uniform pellet distribution with highest pellet counts in the center (17.2-inch diameter) and middle (24.5-inch diameter) portions of the pattern.

45 yards	Trap 8	Mod	24 inches
	* Trap 8	Full	24 inches
	Trap 7½	Full	24 inches

*Trap 8s and full choke is best here, based upon pellet density and uniform distribution in both the center (17.2-inch diameter) and middle (24.5-inch diameter) portions of the pattern. The efficiency of this load/choke combination up to this yardage is evidenced by its popularity with trap shooters.

| 50 yards | * Trap 8 | Full | 17 inches |
| | Trap 7½ | Full | 17 inches |

*Trap 8s produced slightly more uniform pellet distribution and higher pellet counts in all portions of the pattern. These two chokes/loads were very close in performance. I am sure that in some gun/choke combinations the 7½ would be a better choice.

During all of the pattern tests and target-breaking tests I was surprised at the uniformity and consistency of the patterns produced by all loads fired through cylinder chokes. Another valuable lesson learned

Most rabbit targets are shot within 30 yards, which makes them ideal prospects for a load of skeet 9s and cylinder bore chokes.

while firing these tests was the importance of judging distances correctly when selecting choke and load combinations. An error of ten yards in estimating target distance could make a considerable difference in choosing the right choke and load combination. Rather than attempt to judge target distance by looking at just the target in flight, locate some mark on the ground under the target's path and estimate the distance to that object. If you are able to identify some fixed object under the target's path you could even use a range-finding device like those used by bowhunters to determine exactly how far away the target is.

I just returned from a sporting clays tournament at Heartbreak Ridge, and on one of the stations we had a pair of overhead targets that came from directly behind us. The targets looked very high because they were midis. I gauged their elevation on a very tall pine tree nearby and used an old Boy Scout trick for measuring heights to determine that the place on the pine tree at the same level as the target was only about sixty feet off the ground, or twenty yards! Several shooters who were trying to decide on full or modified chokes asked me what I was using. I told them cylinder and skeet 9s—they looked at me like I was lying through my teeth. I wasn't. I broke 10 out of 10 on the first day and 9 out of 10 on the second day. If I hadn't realized they were midis and used the Boy Scout measuring trick for estimating heights, I too would probably have used a very tight choke and number 8 shot, because those targets really appeared much higher than they actually were.

If I had chosen modified choke and trap 8s, my gun would have produced a thirteen-inch pattern at 20 yards. Skeet 9s in a cylinder choke produce a twenty-four-inch pattern in my gun at 20 yards. This is a good example of the importance of knowing what your gun does at various distances, and the necessity of being able to gauge distances accurately.

You do not have to fire hundreds of test patterns to decide which load and choke pattern is best for your gun. You might want to use my optimum chokes and loads as a starting place and test a few other combinations for comparison. Testing chokes and loads to identify optimum patterns was not the drudgery I expected it to be when I began this book. To be perfectly honest, it was quite interesting most of the time, because I was always finding little surprises and learning new things about my gun and what comes out of the muzzle. I have owned many shotguns since I got my first one forty years ago, but because of the extensive testing I have done for this book, this old Lightning gun I am now shooting is the first one that has really been mine.

7

SHOOTING TIPS FOR EACH FIELD

•

It would be impossible to provide specific information on how to shoot every possible sporting clays field because the possibilities for individuality are virtually unlimited. Most courses change their targets every week or so by moving traps or shooting stations so that the targets continue to be a challenge. But there are a number of fields common to many courses, and success on these fields can be attributed to having a basic understanding of the best technique for attempting specific types of targets.

Driven Grouse

The driven-grouse field at Heartbreak Ridge is named "Kamikaze Grouse." That title is an accurate description of most driven-grouse fields. They come low, they come fast, and they usually pass right over your head.

At the USSCA National Championships at Game Hill, this field was called the "Prairie Chicken," but it had all the characteristics of a driven-grouse. There was a true pair launched from a trap that was out of sight and just over the crest of a hill. The shooter was positioned in a pit blind. It was not unlike shooting a true pair out of the low house from station 8 on a skeet field. Many shooters only fired a total five or six

Cheng Ma is about to break a pair of incoming driven grouse on the
Kamikaze Grouse field at Heartbreak Ridge.

89

shots at the five pairs on this field. By the time they shot the first target, the second had already passed over their heads and was lost.

It is important to take the first target as fast as possible on this rapidly approaching incoming pair. Eye focal points should be at the precise location where the target is first visible, with the gun hold-point below the eye focal point. These are targets that must be taken with no apparent forward allowance, the high-speed gun swing providing the necessary lead. Track them from behind, shoot right at the first target, and repeat the same technique on the second. He who hesitates has lost—one if not both targets!

When shooting a true pair of these fast incoming targets, it is imperative that you decide which target you will shoot first. The targets are often flying very close together when first viewed by the shooter; therefore, you must be focused and concentrating upon the target you will shoot first. You do not have a lot of time to gaze at the pair or decide which one to shoot first after they are flying.

When driven grouse are flying low, close, and fast, cylinder chokes and number 9 shot are the best medicine.

Springing Teal

Generally, this target is thrown nearly straight up. Usually this is either a simultaneous pair or a report pair. Occasionally you will see single springing teal, but it is not too common. On many courses the teal will not be exactly straight up, but will angle slightly away from you. The teal that angles slightly away from you at the peak of its flight usually requires a little more choke because it will be edge-on as it travels away from you. Springing-teal targets that angle away from you at the top of their flights should be broken on the way up. These angling-away targets can become very difficult after they have leveled off and then start to fall, offering the shooter just the edge of the target to hit. Not only are you confronted with minimal target surface to hit, these are very tough targets to read accurately.

When thrown as a true pair, the targets will split near the top of their flights, with one target going left and the other right. Before you take your turn at springing teal, observe which target goes the highest. You will want to shoot the highest climber second. Take the target with the lowest apex first, because it will begin to fall first. Your scores will be higher on this station if you attempt to take both targets on the rise or at the precise moment they stop their ascent.

Once a teal has paused at the top of its flight it will begin to fall and rapidly increase speed until it strikes the ground. It is difficult for most shooters to gauge the velocity of falling-teal targets, which usually results in a desperate attempt at spot shooting; this is unsuccessful more often than not. The teal targets that fall straight down are also very susceptible to being blown about by the wind as they are descending.

Another characteristic to look for as you observe the teal is whether or not one of the targets is obscured by foliage either on the way up or down. If one of the targets does become obscured at some time during its flight, you need to plan your break-points and shooting sequence accordingly. You cannot break a target you cannot see.

One of the more common errors on this field is holding your gun too low when calling for the target. Your gun hold-point should be very near where you expect to break the target. Since this target is usually going almost straight up, it loses velocity rapidly. If you begin to track teal with your muzzles just after it leaves the trap, you will probably shoot over it. This miss will be because if you begin to track a teal right out of the trap, you will be swinging your muzzles after a very fast target (especially if it is a single) that will have slowed down considerably by the time you swing through it and pull the trigger. If you use the high gun hold-point I have suggested, the target will not be traveling as fast when you track it, and there will be less chance of error in swinging through it. Remember, your gun is probably set up to shoot slightly high, so keep your gun moving through the target and you can fire just as you swing through the target.

After breaking the first teal, swing immediately to the second target. Because this target is by now traveling slower than the one you just shot, it may even be about to stop entirely before plummeting back down, so shoot it just as the muzzles begin to overtake the bottom edge. Shooting the second teal should also be attempted before it reaches the peak of its flight, if possible.

There is another method of shooting teal you may want to try. Gale Davis, sporting clays instructor, All America Sporting Clay shooter, and

91

Ken Gagnon exhibits good form with a high gun hold-point prior to
calling for a pair of springing teal at the Minnesota Horse and Hunt
Sporting Clays course.

director of Heartbreak Ridge Sporting Clays, has a unique way of shooting teal that he showed me when I was taking lessons from him. Gale
"rifle shoots" those springing-teal targets thrown straight up. Contradic-
tory to other shots in sporting clays, where looking at the bead is strictly
taboo, he actually aims the gun right at the targets as they pause at the
top of their ascents. He rifle-shoots the first target of a springing-teal
pair and then immediately points right at the second and shoots it. He
shoots the second target like it is a chip off the first. The second target is
taken very quickly. This technique is used only when the springing-teal
targets are launched straight up. If the targets are angling away from the
shooter, this method will probably not be very successful.

Gale's method is not "spot shooting," which is shooting at some spot in front of a moving target in hopes that the target and shot will arrive at that location simultaneously. He is shooting directly at these targets while they are relatively motionless at the peak of their flight, before they begin to fall rapidly back to earth.

Tower or Overhead Shot

These overhead targets have a variety of names. When they come from behind the shooter they are often called ducks, pigeons, or doves. When they approach from in front of the shooter they are usually called driven pheasant.

Mention a hundred-foot tower and you can see jaws tighten and faces go pale. Many new shooters are easily intimidated by their first few experiences at tower-thrown targets. This usually leads to the gunner getting very deliberate and pointing a dead gun out in front of the targets and attempting to check and see if he has enough forward allowance.

That target launched from a hundred-foot tower is less than thirty-five yards off the ground! Thirty-five yards is not a long shot. It just looks farther away. Overhead targets appear to be farther away than they really are, and most are missed because the shooter gets intimidated and gets way in front, tries to see a lead, and then misses. Most of these misses are behind the target. So he tries to see even more lead, checks more carefully, and still misses because in all this checking, measuring, and attempting to guesstimate a 12½-foot lead, he has allowed his muzzles to stop swinging.

Avoid selecting a gun hold-point too close to the tower. If you have a gun hold-point that is too close to the tower, then you will track the target too long and begin measuring and checking lead, which will result in a stopped swing and a dead gun. Select a gun hold-point that allows you to watch the target and read its line. Give the shot time to develop. Let the target pass your muzzles, track it from behind, swing through, and break it.

You must be patient on incomers. Give the target time to stabilize in speed and direction. Don't mount the gun until you are ready to shoot it.

93

Gale Davis *(left)* assumes the traditional ready position as he waits for a high outgoing overhead pair.

Right: When Gale hears the trap launch the target, he exaggerates his backward lean and tips his head as far back as possible. This allows him to see the target much quicker than with the traditional ready position in the previous photograph. Seeing the target quicker gives more opportunity to get a more accurate estimation of speed and angle.

Outgoing Overhead Targets

When the targets come from behind, it is important to have your weight on your rear foot when calling for the target. As the target passes over your head and goes away, you will naturally shift your weight onto your forward foot. If you consistently shoot behind this target, then you are probably not shifting your weight to your front foot while tracking the target with the muzzles. While in your ready position, waiting for

94

the target to appear over your head, the heel of your stock should be just below your shoulder with the muzzles pointing almost straight up and at the point at which you expect the target to pass over your head.

Tip your head backward so you can see the target as soon as possible. After calling for a target that will pass overhead from behind, Gale Davis exaggerates tipping his head backward and leans farther back to see the target quicker. This extreme backward tipping of his head and leaning is awkward and is only done after he hears the trap launch the targets. His technique allows viewing of the targets much quicker than by simply standing straight up and tipping the head back slightly.

Gale introduced me to this technique on one of my trips to Heartbreak Ridge when I was on a station that had a simultaneous pair coming from behind and passing directly overhead. The advantage of maximum tipping of the head and extreme backward lean after hearing the target being launched was considerable. The targets appeared to be traveling about half as fast as when I leaned way back and tipped my head as much as possible. This is a very stressful position, but you will only be in it for a short period of time.

Care should be exercised when mounting your gun on this station. Make sure you mount it by extending the left hand, and avoid a lot of right-hand force. If you muscle the gun to your shoulder with the right hand, it will cause the barrels to seesaw and you will shoot under the target. Wait for the target to pass your muzzles before mounting the gun; this will force you to track it from behind and swing through it rather than poke ahead and spot-shoot.

Once the gun is mounted properly, weight shifts to the front foot and you fire just as the muzzles pass through the target. If the target has started to fall rapidly by the time you catch up with it, you may need to see a little daylight under it. In an effort to obtain a little more lead on this target, some shooters focus on the front edge and shoot just as the muzzles pass that edge as they swing smoothly from behind and through the target.

When shooting an overhead pair from behind, it is usually a good idea to take the first target as quickly as possible, while it is still almost directly overhead and slightly in front. The longer you wait on these outgoing overhead shots, the more difficult they are to break. A target that is directly overhead exposes maximum surface area; as it gets farther

On outgoing overhead shots use an almost vertical gun hold-point and mount the gun by thrusting the fore end forward with your left hand.

away from you, only the edge of the target is exposed to your shot pattern. A quick shot on the first clay also allows more time to read and track the second.

There are several considerations when deciding which target to take first. If one of the pair is dropping more rapidly than the other, take the fast-dropper first. If trajectories are about the same, I like to take the more straightaway of the two first. The straightaway will be more predictable and easier to shoot quickly than the one that is angling away. If one of the targets is considerably ahead of the other, take the rear one first.

Incoming Overhead Targets

If the overhead targets are coming from in front of you, then start with the weight on your front foot. The eye focus point should be in that area where the target is first visible. The gun hold-point should be slightly under the eye focus point. Avoid the temptation to mount your gun too quickly on this station. Give the target time to stabilize both in speed and direction before attempting to break it. Track the target and read the line with your eyes, but avoid mounting the gun until just before the target approaches the target break-point.

The target break-point should be out in front of you, just before the target passes over your head. Be patient on these incoming overhead shots, especially when they come from a considerable distance. If you begin to track the target too early with your muzzles, rather than with just your eyes, you will invariably make the mistake of getting the muzzles out in front of the target too soon, checking the bead, and measuring forward allowance. This will lead to stopping and starting your swing and invariably will cause you to miss.

On singles or a report pair, you can shoot both targets in about the same location. If you are shooting a true pair, then focus on one target at a time and break it before even looking at the second. This is often hard for new shooters to do because the targets are close together when viewed from a distance. Obviously, if you have a true pair, then you must shoot the first bird far enough out in front to allow time to track and break the second before it passes over your head.

Clay targets are the most fragile when struck by shot on the under-

Bob Davis is waiting for a very low outgoing pair that will pass slightly to his right. He has positioned his feet and gun hold-point out toward the target break-point and has turned only his head back toward the trap to see the targets as soon as possible.

Woodcock fields usually feature targets that fly close and quick through trees and vegetation. These targets require open chokes, skeet shells, and a lightning-quick swing.

side. Pellets then cannot bounce off. The concave cup of the target's underside directs all pellets into the target, providing for a maximum expenditure of energy. Taking these targets as nearly as possible directly overhead greatly increases your chances of breaking them because you have a double advantage of maximum surface area and maximum vulnerability. This condition allows you to use a more open choke and smaller shot, which increases your optimum pattern size. I rarely use anything larger than skeet 9s or chokes tighter than improved cylinder on any target that passes directly over my head.

Make sure you know which target is being thrown on all tower and overhead stations. It is difficult to distinguish midis from standards when they are flying overhead.

Don't get careless on this station just because the targets are highly visible and usually in view for relatively long periods of time. Read the target line and read it precisely. Track the target from behind and follow through. Many shooters stop their guns and shoot behind these overhead targets. The most common mistakes on overhead shots are

99

mounting the gun too early and checking measuring leads. Avoid spot-shooting. Track the target from behind, swing through, and keep the gun moving. See some space in front of the target if necessary, but don't try to estimate an exact 3 feet, 9¾ inches lead.

Woodcock Fields

Woodcock fields are usually accurate duplications of woodcock flight and habitat, so you can expect close crossing targets in somewhat thick vegetation. This is a field where skeet shooters, skeet shells, and skeet chokes do well.

As a general rule, these targets are taken close and quick. Eye focal points and gun hold-points are close to the trap. This is the type of field where the British style of mounting your gun during the tracking of and swinging through the target is imperative. Execute a sloppy seesaw gun-mount or take your eyes off the target to check the bead for forward allowance and you will have a lost target.

Many shooters do not dismount their guns for the second shots on report pairs on this station. I think that is a mistake, especially where the targets are fairly low. Having that gun already mounted contributes to a jerky initiation of swing and can even obscure your view of the target. It takes longer to correctly read a target, even a close, fast one, than to mount your gun. On report pairs, dismount the gun between shots.

On a true pair of woodcock, you may have to keep the gun mounted if the targets fly out of view quickly. If confronted with this situation, shoot the rear target first and keep the muzzles moving to break the front target. Any time you shoot a front target first, you must either wait for the second target to go past your muzzles, attempt a spot shot, or, worst of all, swing your muzzles back toward the trap, stop the muzzles, then start the muzzles in the opposite direction to track the target. All three are fraught with risk.

Because true doubles on this station often fly very close together, it is tempting to look at both targets and then shoot between them. Focus on one target, in this case the rear one, and break it. When you get right down to dealing with reality, there are no doubles in sporting clays, trap, or skeet. There are only singles flying at the same time! Look at them,

Avoid the temptation to look at both targets in a true pair. Focus on the rear bird first, break it, and then focus on the remaining target and break it, too. Sounds easy—but it's tough to do.

concentrate on them, shoot them—one at a time. If you break two close-flying targets on one shot it should be a surprising bonus.

I have a good friend, Cheng Ma, who is considerably above the average sporting clays shooter. One of Cheng's great joys in life is to break two targets with one shot. But this is something he works at, and he only attempts the trick when he has looked at a lot of targets on a station and knows where the targets will be close enough to each other to break together.

I saw several competitors at the USSCA Nationals Championships not take a second shot at a pair because they thought they had broken both targets with one shot. They saw fragments of the first target that they mistakenly believed came off both targets. They were wrong, and the second target enjoyed a long stable flight until it finally fell to earth to be declared "lost" by the referee. Even if you think you have broken both targets with one shot, continue to swing and shoot at the biggest piece you can see. That biggest piece may well be the second bird you

101

thought you had broken, but didn't. Even if you did break them both, busting a fragment of a broken target is an impressive trick when you pull it off. The real advantage to firing both shots is that you will reduce the chances of losing a target you thought was broken by your first shot.

Some shooters advocate firing two shots at a target if they miss it the first time. I think this is a tactical error. It is quite possible to break a small chip off the first target that you do not see, but the referee does. When you shoot that first target again, you succeed in breaking the same target twice, which only adds up to one target on your score sheet. Taking the time to determine if you broke the first target will delay reading the second target and breaking it. This delay, however slight, will reduce your chances of breaking the second target in the pair.

You can expect to have woodcock targets pass behind some obstacle and reappear as they come out the other side. It is quite common to see shooters fire at these targets while they are behind such an obstacle. It is impossible to focus on the targets and watch an obstacle at the same time. The best way to avoid shooting at a target as it goes behind a tree is to set up your gun hold-point and eye focal points so that you will not be overtaking the target as it goes behind the obstacle. If you are shooting a pair that pass behind an obstacle, shoot the rear target before the obstacle and the other target as it emerges. If you select the correct gun hold-points and eye focal points, then you will avoid firing a shot charge into a tree or thick vegetation on woodcock fields.

Rabbits

Rabbit fields generate more "chin music" than any other field on a sporting clays course. It is startling to see a clay target rolled along the ground for the first time. Bolting-bunny targets will leap into the air, duck behind stumps, and dive into depressions with the same unpredictability of their flesh-and-blood namesakes. The only thing consistent about rabbit targets is their inconsistency. It is quite possible, and very probable, to stand on a station and have each of ten consecutive rabbit targets do something different.

Since rabbit targets make frequent contact with the ground, they are continually changing speed and direction. Because of this constant state of change, it is a very good idea to avoid tracking a rabbit target too long

102

with the muzzles of your gun. Pick them up as early as possible with your eyes, but avoid mounting your gun until the target is very near the target break-point. This is a field where it is extremely important to set yourself up correctly and have your feet positioned to allow maximum follow-through at the target break-point.

After viewing targets and deciding upon your target break-point, select an eye focal point that allows you to see the target at the earliest possible moment. You must read this target and respond to what it does. Do not try to anticipate or predict what this target will do or where it will do it. Don't convince yourself that just because the shooter before you had ten targets bounce in the air that you will have ten targets bounce in the same place. I have already mentioned that frequent contact with the ground will affect target behavior; target impact upon the ground will also cause minor changes in the surface of the course where the rabbits travel. Shot charges fired into the ground also will change the features of the surface, causing targets to rebound in a different manner than their predecessors.

Look at the targets, study what they do, and be prepared for similar behavior. But do not step up to this station with the idea that you know exactly what the targets will do. After selecting target break-points, eye focal points, and gun hold-points, your mind should be blank and all your actions should be based on what the target is doing, not what you thought it was going to do.

I have emphasized several times the importance of keeping the muzzles under the target's path and seeing the target on top of the rib. This is extremely important when shooting bolting rabbits. Make sure your gun hold-point is below the rabbit's path when you call for the target.

The low gun-hold on this field provides several advantages. The most important is that you won't hide the target with your barrels. A low gun-hold will allow you to see and break the target that doesn't bounce in the air. If the rabbit does leap, then all you have to do is lift your muzzles and bust him in the air.

Many new shooters fear a leaping rabbit. Experienced shooters love airborne bunnies because they know a rabbit target is most predictable and consistent while it is in the air and that is the easiest place to break them. It is risky to track a rabbit and hope it will bounce, because it may just roll merrily along and never leave the ground. Don't wait for a

103

You must focus 100 percent on rabbit targets, watch what they do, and don't anticipate bounces. Many a shooter has lost a rabbit target because he waited for a bounce that never happened. (Note the barrier created with hay bales along the rabbit route.)

bounce, but do take advantage of them when they occur.

Your gun hold-point on this station will usually be very near the target break-point. As I have already emphasized, you cannot track this target very long with your muzzles because changes in direction and speed are almost constant. Let the target pass your muzzles, swing through the target, and shoot right at it. Don't try to lead or spot-shoot. It is very difficult to shoot out in front of a rabbit target when you don't really know for sure where it is going! Swing fast and shoot right at the target in the air or rolling on the ground.

If targets are extremely fast or are visible over a long distance, shoot them as late as possible. This will allow them to slow down some and will also reduce somewhat the extreme angles to which they will bounce.

Since most sporting clays fields are designed to mimic shots offered by game in the field, rabbit targets are usually fairly close-range propositions. If the targets are 25 yards or less, go to skeet 9s and cylinder bore chokes.

Fur and Feather

Another popular field on most courses is the fur and feather, which features a combination of rabbit and aerial targets. These are usually

This shooter has correctly positioned his feet and gun hold-point out toward the target break-point and turned only his head back toward the eye focal point.

This shooter has just broken the rabbit portion of the fur and feather and is waiting for the aerial target crossing from right to left to appear.

report or following pairs. In most cases the rabbit is launched first, followed by a flushed grouse. On occasion the flushed bird may be launched first, followed by a bolting rabbit.

On any fur and feather field, you must focus upon each individual target. Don't worry about the second target until after you break the first one. Don't rush the shot on your first target of a report pair; the second one won't be launched until you shoot the first one. It is a very good practice to dismount your gun between these two shots, especially if the rabbit is launched second.

Suggestions for Shooting Doubles

There are a few general rules that apply to shooting simultaneous pairs. There are exceptions to these rules if one target falls faster, goes

106

behind an obstacle, or passes out of range before its mate. But in most situations where true pairs are encountered, a few basic rules will increase scores.

Whenever feasible, shoot the rear target of a true pair first, then keep the muzzles moving and shoot the front target. On an outgoing pair with one target going straight away from you and the second angling to the right or left, some shooters prefer to shoot the straightaway first and then swing to the angling target. This works pretty well if the targets are fairly high and not widely split.

You might want to consider another alternative if the targets are on a low trajectory and/or widely split. In this case there are advantages to right-handed shooters taking the right-hand target first and left-handers taking the left-handed target first. The rationale for this technique is based on several basic shooting principles. With a mounted gun, a right-handed shooter can see that second target easier if it is to his left. It is harder for a right-handed shooter to see the second target if it is on his right because the gun will obscure his vision and often cause him to lift his head off the stock to see the target. Right-handed shooters also tend to swing smoother and maintain positive head contact on the stock when they are swinging from right to left. Just the opposite is true for left-handers; they should take the left target first and then swing toward the target on the right.

If a true pair is widely divided, don't hesitate to shift your feet to take the second target. Position your feet to break the first target and then move your feet to break the second, or your body will bind up as you try to swing wide on the second bird and this will surely make you miss.

When shooting report pairs, it is best to dismount your gun between the two targets. Shoot the first target, look to the eye focal point for the second target, dismount your gun as you are swinging back to the gun hold-point for the second target, see the target, read the target line, mount and swing on the target, and break it.

Dropping Targets

Fields that feature dropping targets are to be expected on just about any sporting clays course and in every tournament. They may be called decoying mallards, settling woodies, or a variety of other names not suitable for publication. I suspect most people think themselves into missing dropping targets. I know I have and probably will again. When dropping targets get within range, most of us watch with dread as they begin to fall and try to calculate where we need to shoot to intercept them as they parachute to earth. Next time you are on a field that features dropping targets, watch the muzzles of other shooters. You will observe as I have that the folks who are consistently missing dropping targets are spot-shooting with a stationary gun.

You will also probably observe that those who are breaking this target are tracking from behind and swinging through the target. If you asked them how much they were holding under these falling targets, they would probably say they are shooting right at them. I had a very hard time making myself track these falling targets and shoot directly at what I knew to be a rapidly falling target. But when I really smoke one of these dastardly droppers, it is because I have used the same good technique that breaks any sporting clays target. Read the line, track it with the muzzles, keep the gun moving, and shoot right at it.

One of the fields that just about drove me nuts when I first started shooting sporting clays, but is now one of my strongest fields, is the dropping target that comes from behind and drops in front of me. Like many new sporting clays shooters, I tried in vain for a long time to intercept these targets by spot-shooting under them.

When I asked Jon Kruger for help on this target he took me out on a regular trap field and positioned me in front of the trap house so that the targets would pass over my head and fall in front of me. He asked me to try a few targets from about 30 yards away, most of which I missed. Then he had me shoot these falling targets at very close range and I broke them consistently. He asked me how much I was leading them. My answer of course was, "I am shooting right at them." Then he moved me a little farther away and told me to do the same thing. I continued to shoot right at them and continued to break them. He kept moving me farther and farther away with the same results. Soon I was breaking these falling targets with regularity at distances from which I had previously been lucky to hit 1 out of 10. Jon told me afterward that I knew how to break the target all along, I just wouldn't let my eye-hand coordination do the job. I was trying instead to guess how far I should hold under the dropping target, and then spot-shoot with a dead gun.

These dropping targets are not falling very fast, and just by tracking them with the gun barrels and keeping the barrels moving as you shoot will take care of any necessary forward allowance.

In most cases these dropping targets are out of range when you first view them. Be patient and wait for the shot to develop. If you have a true pair, shoot first the one falling fastest. If they are falling at pretty much the same speed, shoot the more distant one first. The first target should be taken quickly enough to give you plenty of time to shoot the second one.

Keep your muzzles up as you wait for dropping targets to come within range, read the target line, track 'em and shoot right at them, and you will be pleased with the results.

Quartering Targets

This is another target that gives not only new shooters, but seasoned hands lots of problems. There was a quartering-away shot at the 1989 USSCA National Tournament that gave everyone fits. This target was launched from the shooter's right and slightly downhill. I can speak with authority on the mistakes made on this field because I made all of them—several times! Many unsuccessful shooters used gun hold-points that were too close into the trap and tracked the targets too long. Another common error on this shot is holding the muzzles too high and seesawing the barrels as the gun is mounted, causing the shot to go low.

Gun movement should be kept at a minimum when shooting quartering shots. They are usually not as far away or traveling as fast as they appear to be. Most people shoot in front of quartering targets. Cheng Ma is as deadly on quartering targets as anyone I have ever seen. He minimizes gun movement and shoots right at them.

Next time you are at a trap shoot or a gun club where some good trap shooters are really cracking clay targets, watch their gun muzzles and see how far they travel on each shot. Since most trap shots are quartering away, the technique is the same for shooting sporting clays targets that are quartering away from you. They don't point their muzzles into the trap house either, do they?

A combination trap and skeet field is a good place to practice quartering-away shots. Stand on skeet field stations 1, 2, 6, or 7 and shoot

109

This outstanding sporting clays shooter, Andy Folsom, is about to break a difficult quartering-away shot that is crossing right to left. His gun hold-point is just to the right of the target break-point. Very little swing is required on quartering-away shots; most shooters track them too far.

targets launched out of the trap house. If you have difficulty from a particular angle, ask the trapper to lock the trap machine in that position until you learn to break the target consistently.

Chukars

These targets are usually launched from a trap downhill from the shooting station. The targets as a rule are either crossing or quartering

110

away from you and falling rapidly. If the targets are crossing in front of you, you will need to select a gun hold-point in close to the trap. If they are quartering away, then select a gun hold-point out closer to the target break-point.

Study this target before you shoot it. They are usually set up to fall rather quickly, so it is easy to shoot over them. Read the target line, track 'em, and shoot right at them while keeping your gun moving. This is one station where I believe you are better off to attempt the shot as quickly as possible.

One of the surprises I encountered when shooting the tests to determine what it took to break a clay target was how indestructible targets were when they were struck on the shoulder between the flat dome and the edge. If you will visualize a target launched below your shooting station and dropping out in front of you, what part of the target will your shot pattern strike? That's right, the shoulder. I am convinced that a target that only exposes the top of its shoulder to a shot charge requires a dense pattern of at least number 8s. I suspect a lot of shooters are choosing open chokes and number nine shot in an effort to make contact with chukar targets. They probably are making contact, but the pellets are too few and not large enough to break a target at the angles presented on most chukar fields. I have only tried this theory at three tournaments, but I have shot my three highest chukar scores in those three tournaments!

Battue

This is another target that strikes fear into many shooters' hearts when they first see them thrown. When flying in an edge-on position to the shooter they are hard to see, nearly impossible to hit, and hard to break when you do hit them on the edge.

That's the bad news. The good news is that they don't stay edge-on to the shooter. As they begin to lose velocity they roll over or curl to the side. When they roll over sideways they are very easy to see, they can be hit, and if you do hit them they are very easy to break when struck by just a few pellets.

Battues begin to plunge earthward very rapidly once they curl over on their sides, so it is a good idea to break them just as soon as possible after they turn broadside to you. As I said in Chapter 6, as unbelievable as it sounds, just two number-9-shot pellets will break a battue to about 50 yards when it is struck broadside.

8

TRAINING AND PRACTICE
FOR COMPETITION

•

Serious participants in golf, tennis, basketball, football, and baseball realize the value of a good coach or instructor. Wingshooting and clay-target shooting schools and instructors are plentiful in England and Europe. Unfortunately, Americans rarely turn to shooting schools or shooting instructors to learn how to shoot shotguns. But in the past few years, interest in shooting schools has been on the increase. Sporting clays shooting clinics are becoming more common as course managers respond to requests from new participants for quality instruction. Even if a course doesn't have enough steam to sponsor one of the big-name instructors, an entry-level course for beginning shooters would certainly attract some local participants.

Ask just about any top competitor in trap, skeet, or sporting clays if he ever took lessons and the answer will probably be a resounding yes. I have observed many top competitors taking lessons from instructors during practice sessions the day before a tournament. I have also seen top shooters return to a field in the evening to practice on a particular target that they had problems with during the tournament. This constant effort to improve is what separates top shooters from everyone else. A good shooting instructor will often cause his student to show remarkable improvement after just a few lessons and some serious practice. Don't expect to take lessons or read a book on sporting clays and achieve major improvements immediately. Shooting is a game of skill that does require regular quality practice sessions. All your instructor can do is give you the right tools—you will have to make yourself a mechanic!

Even if you do not intend to enter world-class sporting clays tournaments, you may want to take some lessons to place higher at local club tournaments or be a better game shot. Any improvements on a sporting clays course will be carried over to game shooting.

Selecting an instructor requires some thought. Do not assume that just because a guy can shoot, he is capable of teaching you to shoot. Many above-average shooters don't know how they shoot. Many good shots use a method that works for them, but they don't understand or know how to teach other methods that may work better for you.

If just being an outstanding performer were the only requirement for being a good coach or instructor, then the coaches in the NFL, NBA, or major-league baseball would all be former stars of the sports. Many of the best professional coaches and instructors were only moderately successful as players, if they played in the pros at all. Many times, the best instructors are those of only mediocre talents who had to study and practice form, technique, foot position, swing, and gun-mount to excel as a

Instructor Gale Davis demonstrates correct technique to several students.

competitive shooter. Obviously, the best coaches are those who are both outstanding shooters and talented teachers. Before you lay out any big bucks for shooting instructions, ask for references and a resumé of the instructor's background and experience.

There are advantages to taking lessons from several different instructors. No two people shoot exactly the same. If you study several different techniques, you will be able to select the methods that work best for you.

When I first got interested in shooting competitive skeet, I ordered three years of back issues of *Skeet Shooting Review* and read every article on how to shoot registered skeet. I photocopied every reference on how the top shooters shot each individual station. I then filed this information by individual station. The most important lesson I learned was that all the top competitors had variations in their technique. There is no single best way to shoot any clay-target sport. There are, however, some basic fundamentals common to all the many varied techniques used by successful shooters.

In addition to taking lessons and practicing on a regular basis, it is a good idea to be a dedicated and persistent student of the game if you ever want to reach your own personal optimum level of performance. The top guns in the sporting-clays game are also the most dedicated students of the sport. Jon Kruger, Dan Carlisle, King Howington, Cheng Ma, Holly Haggard, and many others are always studying the game and searching for ways to surpass their own personal-best performances. They are continuously experimenting, reading shotgun publications, and learning from other shooters.

As you shoot in a few tournaments, you will be able to identify certain types of targets that give you trouble. Keep a record of your scores and concentrate on practicing on those stations. Even though no two fields are the same, there are certain categories of targets to be identified and worked on. You may have trouble with rabbits, simultaneous pairs, tower targets, long quartering-away shots, overhead crossers, falling targets, battues, chukar fields. Keep a record of your scores and soon you will be able to identify the types of targets that produce your lowest scores. Once you have identified the types of targets that are problems for you, plan a training schedule to practice on those priority targets and put that plan in writing. This training plan should include schedule,

115

Practice sessions should be serious—with specific goals and objectives to be accomplished.

number of practice targets, and a method of objectively evaluating progress.

A sample training plan could look like this example.

TRAINING PRIORITY *Springing Teal*

OBJECTIVE:

To increase percentage on springing teal from 50 percent to 75 percent

BASIC TECHNIQUE:

Study books and magazines for suggestions on various techniques for shooting springing teal.

Take lessons on how to shoot springing teal.

Select springing teal technique to be used.

TRAINING SCHEDULE

DATE	SKILL SEGMENT AND PRACTICE LOCATION
1/3/90	Shoot fifty springing teal practice targets concentrating on gun hold-points, eye focal points, and target break-points.
	After completing springing-teal practice, shoot a practice round on the entire course.
	COURSE: Pigeon Mounting Sporting Clays
1/6/90	Shoot twenty springing-teal practice targets. Change trap spring tension and shoot twenty springing teal. Move to another station and shoot twenty springing teal. Change trap spring tension again and shoot twenty targets. Increase distance from target and shoot twenty springing teal.
	COURSE: Wolf Creek
1/7/90	Shoot fifty springing-teal practice targets, concentrating on gun hold-points, eye focal points, and target break-points.
	After completing springing-teal practice, shoot a practice round on the entire course.
	COURSE: Cherokee Rose Plantation
1/10/90	Shoot twenty springing-teal practice targets. Change trap spring tension and shoot twenty springing teal. Move to

117

another station and shoot twenty springing teal. Change trap spring tension again and shoot twenty targets. Increase distance from target and shoot twenty springing teal.
COURSE: Wolf Creek

1/13/90   Shoot 100 springing teal targets.
COURSE: Pigeon Mountain

1/14/90   Shoot 100 springing teal targets.
COURSE: Wolf Creek

TRAINING PROGRESS EVALUATION TO BE COMPLETED BY 1/31/90

Shoot three rounds of sporting clays, including all fields for score. These evaluation rounds should all be shot on different courses and during tournaments if possible. Compute average of springing-teal scores to see if training objective of 75 percent has been achieved. If training goals are met, focus on new training priority. If goals are not met, take a refresher training session with instructor to identify specific problems and prepare new training schedule.

It may not be possible for you to get to the nearest sporting clay facility as often as you would like. By using a little imagination and ingenuity it is possible to improvise sporting clays practice fields. Many sporting clays fields can be duplicated on conventional trap and skeet fields, if those are the only facilities available to you for practice, simply by shooting from locations other than the stations normally used in those sports. If you are having trouble with falling targets, stand behind station 2 or 3 on a skeet field and shoot high-house targets as they begin to fall. You can lock a trap machine and shoot outgoing targets from skeet stations 1 and 7 to practice on high quartering-away shots. I have even seen people stand on the steps of a skeet high house and practice the chukar-type targets, which are often launched downhill from the shooter in tournaments.

If you don't have a trap or skeet field all to yourself and have to practice in a squad with other shooters, you can still get quality sporting clays practice by shooting conventional targets from the usual positions. Ask the puller to delay releasing the target for up to three seconds after your call, and keep your gun off your shoulder until you see the target.

118

Instructor Holly Haggard loads the two traps mounted on elevators at her training facility. Her students call the structure "Babel Tower." She is known to her friends as "Lady Holly, Duchess of Babel Tower."

When shooting stations 1 and 7 on a skeet field, let the outgoing targets get to the opposite side of the field before attempting to break them if you are having trouble with long dropping shots. Another good practice shot can be taken from skeet field station 8 by turning your back to the house and letting the target pass over your head from behind. You can even ask the puller to throw your targets as report pairs rather than singles. You get the idea. The only limits for improvising sporting clays practice is your own imagination.

To practice those long crossing shots, simply stand behind skeet stations 3, 4, and 5. You will be surprised at how much more forward allowance is required from just ten feet behind one of these stations.

Another way to practice sporting clays is to get a few of the inexpensive portable machines and set up practice stations of your own. I have several of these, plus a Champion ET Trap. With this combination I can duplicate most fields. The Champion ET is my real workhorse because it throws rabbits, simultaneous doubles, and has the ability to just about throw a target into the next county. I made a springing-teal field simply by attaching a small portable trap to the side of a stump vertically.

Another solution for quality sporting clays practice is stick birds. Stick birds are simply clay targets launched from hand-throwers that have extension handles to put more speed on the targets. With a little practice you can pitch some rather interesting targets with a stick-bird thrower. I suggest you spend the small difference in price and get a high-grade stick-bird thrower that is built on golf-club shafts from Jim White (Route 4, Box 1358, Cairo, Georgia 31728) rather than one of the plastic discount-store jobs. Jim makes stick-bird throwers in four different lengths.

Stick birds are enjoyable to shoot, but they can be very dangerous. An experienced stick-bird thrower can throw a clay target in excess of one hundred miles per hour. Protection in the form of barriers that will stop a clay target are required for all shooters and spectators. A target may come out of the stick before or after the thrower expects it to and inflict serious injury to shooters or spectators. I once saw a spectator hit in the face with a clay target, and he looked as if he had been hit with a baseball bat. The last word I got on him was that he would lose the sight of one eye. If you are throwing stick birds, there must be barriers to protect both shooters and spectators from wild throws. It should be obvious that barriers are also present when shooting stick birds to prevent the shooter from swinging his gun toward the thrower or any spectators.

Most of the superior sporting clays shooters I know practice gun mounting on a daily basis. You don't have to practice two hundred gun-mounts at a time to achieve measurable progress. Just twenty-five practice gun-mounts in the morning and evening will produce obvious progress in just a week or two. Avoid looking directly at the barrels or bead when practicing gun-mounts; your eyes should be focused on an imaginary target on the wall. I have several mini targets attached to the wall of my basement where I do my practice gun-mounts. You can also mount and swing on imaginary clay targets. These imaginary targets can be crossers, incoming, overheads, rabbits, or just about anything else you want them to be.

The Soviets won more medals than any other country in the 1976 Olympics. The East Germans were second. These two countries were so dominant that many sports fans suspected they had discovered some miracle drug to elevate personal athletic performance. Since no such

A major portion of each practice session should address specific targets that give you trouble. Also, practice the mental aspects of the game. Get your mind right before calling for targets. Focus on every practice target just as if it was the biggest tournament of your life.

drug was ever detected in testing of the athletes, many assumed it was also impossible to detect in a blood or urine test. Later, after the secret was shared with the rest of the athletic world, it was discovered that the key to those ultimate athletic performances was not drugs, but mental training. In his excellent book, *Peak Performance,* Dr. Charles A. Garfield explains methods anyone can use to attain personal peak-performance levels.

The Peak Performance training program involves motivational analysis, goal-setting, developing primary skills, controlling concentration and physical intensity, mental rehearsal, maintaining peak-performance feelings, and letting yourself go during competition. The scope of this book does not allow an in-depth explanation of Dr. Garfield's Peak Performance methods. So I urge you to read his book and find out for yourself how to attain optimum personal performance shooting sporting clays.

Setting personal goals is one of the most important things a shooter who wants to improve personal performance can do. Goals should be realistic, but also challenging. It may be nothing more than just moving up to a higher class or attaining a major achievement such as placing in your class at a national tournament.

Obtaining major personal goals is a lot like eating an elephant: You have to do it one bite at a time. After establishing your major sporting clays goals, set some short-range goals to insure major goal achievements. Establish a training or practice schedule and stick to it. Schedule participation in smaller tournaments to gain experience in competition. As I have already mentioned earlier in this chapter, I believe it is important to schedule a tournament early in your competitive career. Going to a big tournament can be a major motivational and educational experience.

9

TOURNAMENT TIPS AND TECHNIQUES

•

I was a hunter for over three decades before I entered my first registered competition, which was a skeet shoot at Palm Beach Trap and
Skeet Club. That first tournament was as exciting as any hunt for live
game. Shooting in competition provides that rush of adrenalin and excitement that just doesn't happen when you are shooting a few casual
targets with friends at your local gun club or sporting clays course.

I competed in rodeos during high school and college. I was on my
college track and football teams. After my college athletic career was
over, I became a spectator. Oh, I hunted and fished with a passion, but I
did not participate in competitive sports. I often longed for the thrill,
excitement, and challenge of my college days. And then I entered a
competitive skeet shoot and my days as a couch potato were considerably reduced. I enjoy shooting sporting clays as much as any game I
ever played. Shooting in a tournament, in my opinion, is the ultimate
sporting clays experience.

If you shoot sporting clays primarily to improve your success on game
during the hunting season, you will find that shooting a few tournaments
during the spring and summer will motivate you to practice on a more
regular basis. Every tournament is like opening day of hunting season.

You don't have to compete against the best shooters when you go to
your first few sporting clays competitions. All tournaments are set up so

123

that you can compete in classes against other shooters of similar ability. Open class, or high overall, winners are those shooters who shoot the highest scores in a particular tournament. Then there are additional classes that may include AA, A, B, C, D, E, Hunter, Novice, or Non-Classified (NC). Your class is determined upon your average in previous registered tournaments. The Hunter Class is offered at most USSCA tournaments and the targets are not registered.

NSCA*			USSCA*	
CLASS	AVERAGES		CLASS	AVERAGES
AA	.90 and over		AA	70 and above
A	.80 to .8999		A	60 to 69.9
B	.70 to .7999		B	50 to 59.9
C	.60 to .6999		C	0 to 49.9
D	.50 to .5999			
E	Below .4999			

*As this is being written, in October 1989, both NSCA and USSCA are considering changes in shooter classifications for 1990.

If you have never competed in a registered tournament, you may be classified in one of several ways. You may be placed in a class with other shooters who have not yet shot enough targets to receive a classification. Or you may be classified upon a portion of the targets during a tournament that are selected at random.

Since participation in sporting-clay tournaments is growing so fast, every tournament has a large representation of non-classified shooters. To give everyone a fair chance of being placed in a class with other shooters of equal ability, shooters are often classified and prizes awarded based upon what is known as the Lewis Class System.

The Lewis System is pretty simple. When all shooting has been completed, the scores are listed in numerical order from the highest to the lowest. They are then divided into as many groups as there are classes. For example, if there were thirty entries and five classes, there would be six scores in each class (thirty divided by five equals six). The highest score in each group of six would be the winner of that class.

Here is a simplified example of how the Lewis Class System works:

Tournament Tips and Techniques

Lewis Class System for Thirty Shooters in Six Classes

85 (Winner Class 1)	61 (Winner Class 4)
83	60
83	58
82	57
81	57
80	56
———	———
79 (Winner Class 2)	55 (Winner Class 5)
78	54
76	53
75	52
73	51
68	48
———	———
67 (Winner Class 3)	
66	
65	
65	
63	
62	
———	

There are additional rules for breaking ties and dividing groups of identical scores that fall on the line between classes, but this should give you a general idea of how the Lewis Class System works.

Another system for classifying non-classified shooters is called the "blind draw." A number of fields will be randomly selected at the beginning of the tournament, or after the first 100 targets in a 200-target competition. Competitors will not know which fields have been selected until after the scores are turned in. These randomly selected stations will be used to classify shooters for that tournament.

In the 1989 USSCA National Tournament, non-classified shooters were classed upon the first 100 targets of the 200-target event. The NSCA National Tournament used the Lewis Class System for all contestants.

If you have never competed in a sporting clays tournament, I urge

There are many classes at major tournaments. Here Sandi Nail, winner of the 1989 NSCA National Tournament Ladies Division, calls for a target at the Duck Tower as Bray Vincent, winner of the Jr. Division, looks over her shoulder.

you to "give it a show," as the British say. The thrill of competition adds considerable excitement to a sport that is already a lot of fun. An upcoming tournament will add that extra motivation to practice during those months when hunting season is still many months away. In addition to added excitement and motivation to practice, you may win some rather substantial prizes.

Many shooters have never entered a registered tournament because they don't believe they have a very good chance to win. You probably won't win a national championship in your first few tournaments. But you could win or place in your class and take home money, trophies, or merchandise. Contrary to what most noncompetitors think, shooters in the lower classes have a very good chance of winning substantial prizes at large tournaments. Carl Hudson pocketed $1,250 for winning the C Class at the 1989 NSCA National Tournament. Carl broke 108 out of 200 targets. Charles Payne won $1,000 at the 1989 USSCA National Championships for a C Class first with 135 out of 200 targets.

After you have entered a few registered tournaments and discovered how exciting and how much fun shooting in registered competition is, you may decide to try your luck in a state or national tournament. I think it is a mistake for someone who seriously wants to shoot registered tournaments to wait until he is "competitive" or a contender for one of the top places before entering a major tournament. You don't get to be a major tournament contender by sitting at home or just shooting a few rounds at the local course. If you are going to be a swimmer, you have to get in the water.

I don't believe there is any such thing as going to a major tournament too early in your career. Any shooter has to participate in several major tournaments to become acclimatized to that adrenalin-pumping rarefied atmosphere found only at the big shoots. Shooting with a few friends on a familiar course is fun, but shooting in a major tournament with the "big guns" like Jon Kruger, Dan Carlisle, Doug Fuller, Jim Jamison, and David Bleha is comparable to a baseball fan dressing out and playing with his favorite major-league team. Just watching these top guns break targets is an educational and motivational experience. Don't just read about what happened at the last major tournament, be a part of it!

Ducks Unlimited sponsors sporting clays tournaments that feature generous prizes. As an example, as this is being written I have on my desk a brochure for a DU sporting clays tournament scheduled for September of 1989. These are the prizes for AA, A, B, and C classes: *Class Champion:* Winchester Pigeon Grade 101 with case and choke tubes, five cases of Winchester Super-Lite shotshells. *Class Second:* Four cases Winchester Super-Lite shotshells and $500 in prizes and merchandise. *Class Third:* Three cases Winchester Super-Lite shotshells and $300 in prizes and merchandise. *Class Fourth:* Two cases Winchester Super-Lite shotshells and $200 in prizes and merchandise.

In addition to these class prizes, there was a Hunters Class for non-classified shooters, three Greenwing classes for youngsters (sixteen to seventeen years old, fourteen to fifteen years old, under fourteen years old), a class for women, plus other cash options. The tournament lasted for two days and the two-hundred-dollar entry fee included all your shells, a cocktail reception, and a banquet.

In addition to Ducks Unlimited tournaments, you may want to participate in one of the many other types of sporting clays competitions that are becoming more frequent in all sections of the country. There may be some courses near you that provide sporting clays league shoots. These shoots are usually held several afternoons or evenings during the week. Minnesota Horse and Hunt Club in Prior Lake, Minnesota, has a popu-

Having a shooting partner to attend tournaments with you can cut down on travel and lodging costs. You'll also have someone to give helpful advice if your "wheels come off" during a tournament.

lar league shoot with nearly four hundred regular participants. If your local sporting clays course doesn't provide league shooting, a suggestion from you may be all it takes to get a league started.

Because the vast majority of sporting clays shooters are not registered tournament shooters, many courses offer fun shoots and throw unregistered targets. One of these unregistered fun shoots would be a good way to begin your competitive endeavors. Though the cash and prizes may not be of major proportions, neither will the pressure and competition.

Tournament costs such as mileage and motel bills can be reduced considerably if you get yourself a shooting partner.

If I am going to a major tournament more than a two-hour drive away, I like to arrive a day early and shoot a practice round on the course. This day of practice allows me to discover for myself what I need to prepare for on the following day when all the targets will count. Just a few surprises that may affect your scores are the terrain upon which the course is located, the location of the sun behind targets, and

128

whether water is available on the course during a hot summer tournament. Do you have the right shoes? Are insects a problem? Experiencing beforehand local weather conditions such as temperature, humidity, and wind will help in choosing the right shooting clothes for the tournament the next day.

When I first started shooting registered skeet, my coach, Dan Mitchell, told me to take in a movie the night before a tournament. He cautioned me against just going to my motel room and shooting targets in my mind all evening. It is also a good idea to avoid the local night life and keep alcohol consumption to a minimum. If you hit the booze too hard the night before and wake up with your hair hurting, your teeth itching, and your tongue asleep, it will be impossible to shoot your best. It is hard to concentrate on hitting a clay target when the sound made by the launching trap is like a train wreck!

Just before I go to bed the night before a tournament, I do like to check my gear and gun bag. I check my bag for shooting glasses, ear protection, shell pouch, gloves, hand towel, and shells. If it is particularly hot, I will get several jugs of Gatorade and ice them down. Getting everything in order allows me to turn in knowing I will have no surprises when I arrive to shoot the next day.

I like to arrive early, several hours before I am due to shoot. Visiting with friends and having plenty of time to make last-minute preparations helps me relax. I am not one of those shooters who has to "pump himself up" mentally for a tournament. I am just the opposite, I get very excited and need to work on relaxing.

Whenever possible, I like to shoot a few practice shots to warm up before shooting targets for score. I avoid counting targets or even getting involved in a friendly competition for lunch or even a soft drink. My warm-up shooting is just that. I am interested in loosening up and getting the rhythm of my swing smoothed out. Basketball players shoot warm-up shots before a game. Baseball players take batting practice and runners take a few starts out of the blocks before a track meet. You won't be allowed to shoot any fields that will be used in competition, but there may be a practice field or some extracurricular layout such as a two-man flush or stick birds where you can bust a few caps and loosen up a bit before getting down to the serious business of breaking targets for score.

This is another tournament technique Dan Mitchell taught me: Relax between shots. Learn to relax mentally when you are not actually on station and shooting. It is difficult to focus on shooting targets for several hours or a full day without relieving mental stress between shots.

When you are walking from one field to another, forget about the targets you dropped on the last station. I have a good friend who is a very good sporting clays shot. He and I have shot together in many tournaments. On several occasions I have seen him miscount his score on a field or shoot badly and then, because his mind is agitated over what happened, he shoots a disastrous score on the next field.

Don't worry about the ones you have missed or some field you are dreading later in the tournament; focus and concentrate on the targets one at a time. The time to think about a target is when you are shooting it! Don't worry about the ones you missed on the last field or some field you have to shoot later. Don't even worry about the last target; the important target is the one you are shooting.

Another mental exercise most experienced shooters agree on is to avoid counting targets. This often has the same disastrous affect on performance as worrying over targets you missed on the last field. Don't count your score or anyone else's. It is a good idea to keep up with your score on each field in case of a mathematical error by the referee. Winners are not chosen on how well they keep score, but on how many targets they break. You have to break 'em one at a time and that is how you must think about them!

When you arrive at a field, the time you spend waiting to shoot should be spent observing targets. Don't just take a casual look at the targets flying through the air. This is the time to gather specific information and decide how you will break the targets. Make sure you know which targets are being thrown. If you are not sure if a target is a standard or midi, ask the referee. Observe where the target is coming from and its line of flight. Decide where you intend to break it. Estimate the range. Is it falling or rising? Where will your eye focus point be? Where will your gun hold-point be?

Jon Kruger taught me another little trick on reading targets. King Howington and I were taking a few days' lessons from Jon at Millrock Gun Club. Jon positioned King and me on a skeet field in the neighborhood of station 5. He then had a target launched from the low house

While you are waiting to shoot, study the targets and make those important decisions concerning target break-points, gun hold-points, and eye focal points. Don't just copy the shooter in front of you; his shooting style may be completely different from yours.

on the adjoining field. At the sound of the trap launching the target Jon began, "One thousand one . . . one thousand two . . . one thousand three . . ." and the target came past the low house on our field. While you are waiting to shoot, count the time-delay between the trap noise and the appearance of the target. This is especially helpful if the trap is concealed a considerable distance from where the target is first visible.

Don't rush the trapper. It is very easy, especially when you have crushed several targets in a row, to reload rapidly and call quickly for your next pair. To throw pairs of targets that fly just like the pair before, a trapper must place the two targets at precisely the same locations on two trap arms. If you rush the trapper, then it is very possible that you may get a much more difficult and widely divided pair. Give the trapper time to place targets precisely. This slower pace will also give you time to focus upon what you have to do to break the next pair. Pace yourself when calling for targets and your scores will be several targets higher at the end of the day.

Another negative mindset that can reduce your scores is worrying about the weather. The same rain is falling on all the shooters and the wind is blowing everyone else's targets just as much as it is yours. You can actually make bad weather work to your advantage. If you don't allow it to bother you, you will have some advantage over those competitors who are focused on the miserable conditions rather than concentrating on each individual target. I love it when everyone else is aggravated with the weather because I refuse to let it bother me.

If the weather is hot, it takes a little more than the right mental attitude to deal with the situation. In addition to telling myself that the temperature is the same for all competitors, I also drink lots of fluids. But stay away from soft drinks and never drink alcohol until the guns are put away!

I perspire a lot in hot weather. In addition to drinking lots of liquids, I also take along a towel and a few bandannas to dry my hands, face, and gun. Sweatbands will keep drops of perspiration from trickling down your face and dropping onto your shooting glasses.

Footwear is an equipment item often overlooked by new competitors. In warm weather I like to wear softball shoes when shooting sporting clays. The rubber cleats provide traction if it rains and help me maintain firm footing if I am shooting on a station on a slope. Sooner or later you

When waiting your turn to shoot, don't stand around holding your gun.
Put it in the rack. The time spent holding an 8 or 9-pound gun when
shooting a hundred-target competition will expend a lot of energy.

will have to shoot on a field with a station that is not level, and those
softball shoes will be worth their weight in broken targets.

It is also pretty good strategy to conserve energy whenever possible. I
think it was Vince Lombardi who said "Fatigue makes cowards of us
all." Fatigue also affects concentration and could slow your swing down
just enough to make you miss that one target you need to win a class
trophy or the shootoff. Keep your supply of shells in a shell bag and only
carry enough in your vest to shoot one station at a time. When you are
waiting for your turn to shoot, sit down, put your gun in the rack, and
relax. That little bit of energy saved in this manner may be just enough
to make the difference of one or two targets in your score for a win at

the end of the day. Any energy conserved will also be a major contribution to your ability to win a shootoff in case of a tie.

I guess every shooter has his or her idiosyncrasies. I like to wear a glove on my left hand when it is hot to absorb perspiration and give me a firm grip on the fore-end of my gun. I don't like to wear a glove on my right hand, but I do like to dry it off with a towel in warm weather. I like to apply powder from a shaving stick to my right cheek to facilitate positioning my face on the stock comb. The powder also reduces apparent recoil by allowing the stock to slide along my face and not pull my cheek with it.

It is a good policy to wear the same type of clothing when shooting in competition and in practice. I have a Bob Allen shooting vest that I wear every time I practice, shoot in a tournament, or even when I am practicing gun-mounts with an empty gun. Since sporting clays is primarily a warm-weather sport for most shooters, many prefer to wear a shooting shirt with a padded shoulder and keep their shells in a shell pouch on a belt.

For headgear, I like a baseball-type cap. This style of shooting cap is probably the most versatile when it comes to keeping the sun out of your eyes, and it can be turned around backwards whenever you attempt a target in which the bill of the cap would obstruct your view, such as with overhead targets coming from behind.

The following checklist is one I keep in my computer. I just run a copy to use for each tournament.

SPORTING CLAYS TOURNAMENT CHECK LIST

DATE _____ LOCATION _____

MOTEL _____

AIRLINE TICKET _____ RENTAL CAR _____

TOURNAMENT INFO AND DIRECTIONS TO COURSE _____

ADVANCE REGISTRATION FOR TOURNAMENT _____

GUN _____ KEYS TO GUN CASE _____ KEYS TO CAMERA CASE _____

SHOOTING BAG _____

SHOOTING BAG CONTENTS

   GLASSES _____ GLASSES CLEANER _____ SHELL POUCH _____

   NOTEBOOK _____ PEN _____ GLOVES _____ BANDANNA _____

   SWEATBAND _____ BAG FOR EMPTIES _____ READING GLASSES _____

Tournament Tips and Techniques

CHOKE TUBES ＿＿＿＿＿ SHAVE POWDER ＿＿＿＿＿ CHEW ＿＿＿＿

VEST ＿＿＿＿ HAND TOWEL ＿＿＿＿＿ ASSOC. M'SHIP CARDS ＿＿＿＿

CLASSIFICATION CARDS ＿＿＿＿＿＿＿ RULE BOOK ＿＿＿＿＿

CARD WITH CHOKE/LOAD DATA ＿＿＿＿＿＿＿＿＿＿＿

SHELLS

FOR PRACTICE ＿＿＿＿ FOR STICK BIRDS ＿＿＿＿ FOR FLUSH ＿＿＿＿

TOURNAMENT SHELLS SKEET 9 ＿＿＿＿ TRAP 8 ＿＿＿＿ TRAP 7½ ＿＿＿＿

RAIN JACKET ＿＿＿ HATS ＿＿＿ SHORTS ＿＿＿ LONG PANTS/SHOOTING ＿＿＿

SHOOTING SHIRTS ＿＿＿＿＿ SOCKS ＿＿＿＿＿ SHOOTING SHOES ＿＿＿＿

EYEGLASSES ＿＿＿＿ EXTRA CONTACT LENSES ＿＿＿＿ SUNGLASSES ＿＿＿＿

BRIEFCASE ＿＿＿＿ CAMERA CASE ＿＿＿＿ CAMERA ＿＿＿＿ FILM ＿＿＿

CHECKBOOK ＿＿＿＿ KNEE BRACE ＿＿＿＿

At the very beginning of each season I like to make up a schedule of the major tournaments I want to compete in. There are several advantages to making your plans well in advance. Early registration insures that you will be able to participate if the shoot is sold out. I nearly missed the U.S. Open Skeet Shoot in Phoenix in 1986 because I didn't preregister until the last minute. Fortunately, I was able to compete due to another shooter canceling.

Scheduling tournaments early also helps prevent business and other conflicts. If you have tournament dates in your calendar, it allows you to identify conflicts in advance and resolve them. Another primary reason for scheduling tournaments early is financial. Plane tickets, motel reservations, and car rentals made well in advance often carry substantial discounts. When you have to shoot on a budget, as I do, this can make a big difference.

When I have a big tournament scheduled, even though it may be months away, I am more highly motivated to practice regularly. Not only do I practice on a regular basis when I have scheduled a major tournament, the quality of those practice sessions is better. It is one thing to go to your favorite course and shoot a few casual rounds with friends, it is something else entirely to go to a course with specific training goals in mind and work on obtaining those goals.

10
SAFETY AND ETIQUETTE

•

The wearing of shooting glasses is probably one of the most accurate IQ tests available. The risk of permanent eye damage from target fragments or rebounding shot pellets is too high to ignore. The Fur and Feather Field at the NSCA Nationals had a large tree trunk on the ground at the end of the rabbit's run. Many shooters fired at the rabbit just as it disappeared behind that log, and on occasion pellets bounced back into the crowd of waiting shooters. The pellets were pretty well spent, but I wouldn't have liked to have been hit in the eye with one. In addition to protecting your eyes, high-quality shooting glasses will dramatically improve your ability to see targets quicker and more clearly, and that is the primary requirement for hitting targets.

I prefer shooting glasses with interchangeable lenses. As a rule, I use the lightest tint possible. If everything appears too bright and I have a tendency to squint or the brightness is uncomfortable, I will shift to a darker lens. Some of the violet or purple lenses will make an orange target appear to almost have neon lights on it.

Ear protection is also something you should wear when shooting any clay-target game. The obvious advantage is to prevent loss of hearing. It is a scientific fact that repeated loud noises such as gunfire cause irreparable hearing damage. I like to wear the soft type ear plugs, for several reasons. One is that they are cheap and I am always losing my ear

Safety and Etiquette

Always wear shooting glasses when shooting any clay-target sport. The incoming targets frequently encountered in sporting clays, and varying light conditions, make eye protection mandatory on some fields. Ear protection will prevent hearing loss and you will still be able to hear most traps launch targets.

Keep conversation low when another shooter is attempting to shoot his targets.

protection. The second reason is that I can still hear the trap noise as a target is launched, which helps me anticipate the appearance of the target when the machine is out of sight, which it usually is.

Actions should be kept open at all times with no shells in the magazine or chamber, except when you are actually on the station, ready to fire. Load only one shell at a time except when shooting doubles or other multiple targets such as a flush. Always open your gun and check it before leaving the firing station or turning back toward spectators or others waiting to shoot.

Use no shot larger than number 7½. Larger pellets may carry past the designated shot-fall zone. Larger pellets maintain more energy when rebounding and increase the danger of injuring a spectator.

Before calling for your targets, be sure your field of fire is clear of other shooters, spectators, trappers, or anything else you do not want to put a load of shot into.

While waiting to shoot, be sure your location does not infringe upon the shooter's field of view. Avoid hovering over the shooter ahead of you as he is trying to shoot. Under no circumstances should a shooter move to a stand until it is his turn to shoot and the previous shooter has left the stand.

Keep conversations at a low volume while others are shooting. There is a tendency, when wearing ear protection, for everyone to speak louder. Be aware of this and keep conversations low.

I recently visited a course that had a "wounded" gun rack back behind one of the shooting stations. It was obvious that the gun rack, made of two-by-fours, had been struck by a charge of shot at very close range and that the shot was directed into an area where other shooters would very likely be standing. I asked what happened. A young shooter had a misfire in his double-barrel shotgun. His father walked to the station and took the gun. The father then proceeded to walk back toward the gun rack, where he opened the double that had misfired. The gun discharged upon opening. This story could have had a very sad ending, but fortunately, no one was injured. Keep all guns pointed downrange until the actions have been opened and all shells removed.

It is difficult to play by the rules if you don't know what they are. If you are planning to compete in a tournament, know what the sponsoring association's rules are. Know what the club rules are where you will be

Safe gunhandling is mandatory
in all shooting sports. BE
SAFE—or BE GONE!

shooting. Most clubs have the rules posted in a prominent place. Many clubs actually hand a copy of the range rules to every shooter when they register. This is an extremely wise practice and one that should be used by more course managers.

Even though it is against the rules, I have seen people close their guns and point them at the targets while another shooter is on station. I have also seen shooters step up onto a station to view targets; this is also forbidden in the rule books.

Common courtesy and basic safe gun-handling rules should always be adhered to when visiting any sporting clays course. If you see someone being unsafe with a gun, say something about it. Embarrassment is their friend—it helps them learn! Safe gun handling is everyone's business, even when the gun is being handled by someone else.

Every shooting station should have barriers to prevent a shooter from swinging his gun back toward the referee, other shooters, or spectators. It is very easy for an inexperienced shooter to get excited and track a target in an unsafe direction.

11

DEVELOPING SPORTING CLAYS
AT YOUR CLUB

•

There are several basic decisions to be made when developing a sporting clays course. In addition to location of fields and stations, decisions must be made concerning safety, available funds, and so on. Since all sporting clays courses are different, how can you evaluate a course once it is finished? How do you determine if your course is too difficult or too easy? If, out of a 100-target event, the winner shoots in the mid 80s and the majority of your shooters hit 50 percent of their targets, then the course is about right.

Too many inexperienced course designers and managers set up one or two fields with targets that are practically unhittable. A crossing midi target at 70 yards is a game of chance rather than a test of skill. Every field should have several shooters with perfect scores in a tournament. If your course has a field or two that no one ever goes straight on, then you need to give serious consideration to changing that field. The real challenge in designing a course is to keep the majority of targets within the range of an improved cylinder choke.

I do not mean to imply that there should not be varying degrees of difficulty between fields. Certainly, some should be more difficult than others. It is much better to offer a variety of targets and varying degrees of difficulty instead of eight easy fields and two fields where every

140

shooter hits one or two targets out of ten. If you offer variety, every shooter will do well on some stations and not so well on others.

It is okay to throw fast targets at close range to simulate flushed quail, woodcock, or grouse. It is also okay to throw these targets in thick cover that duplicates natural habitat where these species are found. But don't throw a close, fast target that is only visible when it passes through an opening the size of a TV screen!

The first field at Rocky Comfort Sporting Clays in Quincy, Florida, has what club manager Jesse Beasley calls a "confidence builder." This incomer comes over a large oak tree directly in front of the station and falls just about straight down on the shooter. It requires no lead and looks like a garbage-can lid as it settles toward the shooter. Difficulty increases on other stations, but success on this first field counterbalances lower scores on more difficult stations.

Landscaping and clearing for a sporting clays course at your club should be minimal and can be as simple as having club members show up with chain saws, axes, and swing blades some Saturday afternoon. Hilltops or the banks of a ravine are natural substitutes for towers.

Many sporting clays clubs in England operate on a traveling circus basis. They get permission from a landowner, haul in portable traps, design a one-time-use course, shoot the course, and load up the traps. If your hunting club has a hunting lease, you may be able to negotiate permission to set up several sporting clays shoots during the off-season. Just remember that clay targets are toxic to hogs, so you don't want to be breaking targets over land that may later be used as hog forage.

Ken Gagnon (P.O. Box 98, Cumberland, Rhode Island 02864) has a sporting clays traveling road show he takes to gun clubs that want to throw sporting clays but that do not have machines or haven't designed a course. Ken brings machines, designs course layouts, trains trappers, and I think he even provides awards.

As this manuscript is going to press, Mike Hampton at NSCA is also putting together a traveling sporting clays show that will feature various types of trap machines, assistance in course design, and tournament management. This operation is scheduled to be used at ten Ducks Unlimited sporting clays tournaments in 1990. For dates on the DU shoots and information on having the NSCA portable sporting clays course come to your club or fund-raiser tournament, contact the NSCA.

A sporting clays course can be built with nothing more than a chain saw to clear a few trees. The trees cut down can be used to construct the barriers on each stand. All you then need is a few traps.

Jim Maier waits for a pair of flushing quail at Wolf Creek. Leaving natural vegetation aids realism and challenge to any sporting clays course.